A

VICTOR LAFEBER

Date:

14TH MARCH 2023

Scripture Keys

SCRIPTURE KEYS
Inspiring word for your journey

Written and compiled by Kathleen Schubitz
Affirmations by Kathleen Schubitz

Published by:
RPJ & COMPANY, INC.
RPJandco.com
Orlando, Florida, U.S.A.

Scripture verses quoted from the King James Bible.

First Edition, 2008
Revised Edition, 2009, 2016
Updated Edition, 2019

ISBN-13: 978-1-937770-34-1
ISBN-10: 1-937770-34-6

Cover and Interior design by Kathleen Schubitz

Cover Image: © kevron2001 - Fotolia.com

Printed in the United States of America.

To all those seeking
freedom
from their past.

Scripture Keys

Compiled by Kathleen Schubitz

Inspiring

words

for your

journey

Table of Contents

From the Author

This book originally began as a scriptural companion to my story of abuse, suffering, and finding freedom. Finding Purpose after Abuse, a tool of empowerment for every survivor and inspiration for all those seeking freedom from a past they'd like to forget, gives hope and inspiration for everyone desiring to be an overcomer. Every child of God can seek truth from God and learn to walk in freedom and victory. It is done with the help of the Lord and choosing to put the past behind and living life for Him every day.

As a reader I encourage you to pray these scriptures over your own life and loved ones until the realization begins to take root. Allow the living Word of God to reveal the true identity of who you are in Christ. Let the truth of God's word permeate deep into your soul until you know that you are His beloved.

Positive affirmations have been included along with each topic for creatively speaking over your own circumstances or life situations.

Enjoy your discovery!

God bless you abundantly!

Kathleen Schubitz

Published by:

RPJ & Company, Inc.

RPJandco.com

Scripture Keys

Abundance

I am abundantly blessed and highly favored!

Psalm 37:11 - "But the meek shall inherit the earth; and shall delight themselves in the abundance of peace."

Jeremiah 33:6 - "Behold, I will bring it health and cure, and I will cure them, and will reveal unto them the abundance of peace and truth."

Matthew 13:12 - "For whosoever hath, to him shall be given, and he shall have more abundance:"

Luke 6:45 - "A good man out of the good treasure of his heart bringeth forth that which is good; and an evil man out of the evil treasure of his heart bringeth forth that which is evil: for of the abundance of the heart his mouth speaketh."

John 10:10 - "The thief cometh not, but for to steal, and to kill, and to destroy: I am come that they might have life, and that they might have it more abundantly."

Ephesians 3:20 - "Now unto him that is able to do exceeding abundantly above all that we ask or think, according to the power that worketh in us,"

Acceptance

I am accepted in Christ!

Psalm 69:13 - "But as for me, my prayer is unto thee, O Lord, in an acceptable time: O God, in the multitude of thy mercy hear me, in the truth of thy salvation."

Acts 10:35 - *"But in every nation he that feareth him, and worketh righteousness, is accepted with him."*

2 Corinthians 5:9 - *"Wherefore we labour, that, whether present or absent, we may be accepted of him."*

2 Corinthians 8:12 - *"For if there be first a willing mind, it is accepted according to that a man hath, and not according to that he hath not."*

Ephesians 1:6 - *"To the praise of the glory of his grace, wherein he hath made us accepted in the beloved."*

1 Peter 2:20 - *"For what glory is it, if, when ye be buffeted for your faults, ye shall take it patiently? but if, when ye do well, and suffer for it, ye take it patiently, this is acceptable with God."*

Afflictions

Greater is He who lives in me...!

Exodus 22:23 - *"If thou afflict them in any wise, and they cry at all unto me, I will surely hear their cry;"*

Job 36:15 - *"He delivereth the poor in his affliction, and openeth their ears in oppression."*

Psalm 18:27 - *"For thou wilt save the afflicted people; but wilt bring down high looks."*

Psalm 22:24 - *"For he hath not despised nor abhorred the affliction of the afflicted; neither hath he hid his face from him; but when he cried unto him, he heard."*

Psalm 116:10 - "I believed, therefore have I spoken: I was greatly afflicted:"

Psalm 140:12 - "I know that the LORD will maintain the cause of the afflicted, and the right of the poor."

Hebrews 11:25 - "Choosing rather to suffer affliction with the people of God, than to enjoy the pleasures of sin for a season;"

Anger
Today, I choose peace!

2 Samuel 12:5 - "And David's anger was greatly kindled against the man; and he said to Nathan, As the LORD liveth, the man that hath done this thing shall surely die:"

Psalm 6:1 - "O LORD, rebuke me not in thine anger, neither chasten me in thy hot displeasure."

Psalm 37:8 - "Cease from anger, and forsake wrath: fret not thyself in any wise to do evil."

Proverbs 15:13 - "A merry heart maketh a cheerful countenance: but by sorrow of the heart the spirit is broken."

Ephesians 4:26 - "Be ye angry, and sin not: let not the sun go down upon your wrath:"

Colossians 3:8 - "But now ye also put off all these; anger, wrath, malice, blasphemy, filthy communication out of your mouth."

Anointing
I am anointed by God!

Luke 4:18 - "The Spirit of the Lord is upon me, because he hath anointed me to preach the gospel to the poor; he hath sent me to heal the brokenhearted, to preach deliverance to the captives, and recovering of sight to the blind, to set at liberty them that are bruised,"

Isaiah 61:1 - "The Spirit of the Lord GOD is upon me; because the LORD hath anointed me to preach good tidings unto the meek; he hath sent me to bind up the brokenhearted, to proclaim liberty to the captives, and the opening of the prison to them that are bound;"

1 John 2:27 - "But the anointing which ye have received of him abideth in you, and ye need not that any man teach you: but as the same anointing teacheth you of all things, and is truth, and is no lie, and even as it hath taught you, ye shall abide in him."

Believe
I believe all things work together for my good!

Genesis 15:6 - "And he believed in the LORD; and he counted it to him for righteousness."

Matthew 8:13 - "And Jesus said unto the centurion, Go thy way; and as thou hast believed, so be it done unto thee. And his servant was healed in the selfsame hour."

Mark 9:23 - "Jesus said unto him, If thou canst believe, all things are possible to him that believeth."

Mark 9:24 - "And straightway the father of the child cried out, and said with tears, Lord, I believe; help thou mine unbelief."

Mark 11:23 - "For verily I say unto you, That whosoever shall say unto this mountain, Be thou removed, and be thou cast into the sea; and shall not doubt in his heart, but shall believe that those things which he saith shall come to pass; he shall have whatsoever he saith."

John 12:46 - "I am come a light into the world, that whosoever believeth on me should not abide in darkness."

Blessings
I am abundantly blessed!

Genesis 12:2 - "And I will make of thee a great nation, and I will bless thee, and make thy name great; and thou shalt be a blessing:"

Numbers 6:24-26 - "The LORD bless thee, and keep thee: The LORD make his face shine upon thee, and be gracious unto thee: The LORD lift up his countenance upon thee, and give thee peace."

Psalm 100:4 - "Enter into his gates with thanksgiving, and into his courts with praise: be thankful unto him, and bless his name."

Proverbs 3:10 - "So shall thy barns be filled with plenty, and thy presses shall burst out with new wine."

Proverbs 10:22 - "The blessing of the LORD, it maketh rich, and he addeth no sorrow with it."

Ephesians 1:3 - "Blessed be the God and Father of our Lord Jesus Christ, who hath blessed us with all spiritual blessings in heavenly places in Christ:"

Body
My body is a temple of the Living God!

Matthew 6:22 - "The light of the body is the eye: if therefore thine eye be single, thy whole body shall be full of light."

Matthew 10:28 - "And fear not them which kill the body, but are not able to kill the soul: but rather fear him which is able to destroy both soul and body in hell."

Luke 12:22 - "And he said unto his disciples, Therefore I say unto you, Take no thought for your life, what ye shall eat; neither for the body, what ye shall put on."

Romans 6:12 - "Let not sin therefore reign in your mortal body, that ye should obey it in the lusts thereof."

Romans 8:13 - "For if ye live after the flesh, ye shall die: but if ye through the Spirit do mortify the deeds of the body, ye shall live."

1 Corinthians 6:20 - "For ye are bought with a price: therefore glorify God in your body, and in your spirit, which are God's."

1 Timothy 4:8 - "For bodily exercise profiteth little: but godliness is profitable unto all things, having promise of the life that now is, and of that which is to come."

Breakthrough
I will breakthrough to my glorious future!

Ecclesiastes 3:3 - "A time to kill, and a time to heal; a time to break down, and a time to build up;"

Acts 26:18 - "To open their eyes, and to turn them from darkness to light, and from the power of Satan unto God, that they may receive forgiveness of sins, and inheritance among them which are sanctified by faith that is in me."

Genesis 12:2 - "And I will make of thee a great nation, and I will bless thee, and make thy name great; and thou shalt be a blessing:"

Child of God
I am a child loved by God!

Numbers 6:24-26 - "The LORD bless thee, and keep thee: The LORD make his face shine upon thee, and be gracious unto thee: The LORD lift up his countenance upon thee, and give thee peace."

Deuteronomy 12:28 - "Observe and hear all these words which I command thee, that it may go well with thee, and with thy children after thee for ever, when thou doest that which is good and right in the sight of the LORD thy God."

Psalm 100:4 - "Enter into his gates with thanksgiving, and into his courts with praise: be thankful unto him, and bless his name."

Proverbs 3:10 - "So shall thy barns be filled with plenty, and thy presses shall burst out with new wine."

Proverbs 10:22 - "The blessing of the LORD, it maketh rich, and he addeth no sorrow with it."

Ephesians 1:3 - "Blessed be the God and Father of our Lord Jesus Christ, who hath blessed us with all spiritual blessings in heavenly places in Christ:"

Chosen

I am a chosen vessel!

2 Chronicles 7:16 - "For now have I chosen and sanctified this house, that my name may be there for ever: and mine eyes and mine heart shall be there perpetually."

Psalm 89:3 - "I have made a covenant with my chosen, I have sworn unto David my servant,"

Psalm 106:5 - "That I may see the good of thy chosen, that I may rejoice in the gladness of thy nation, that I may glory with thine inheritance."

Proverbs 22:1 - "A GOOD name is rather to be chosen than great riches, and loving favour rather than silver and gold."

John 15:16 - "Ye have not chosen me, but I have chosen you, and ordained you, that ye should go and bring forth fruit, and that your fruit should remain: that whatsoever ye shall ask of the Father in my name, he may give it you."

1 Peter 2:9 - "But ye are a chosen generation, a royal priesthood, an holy nation, a peculiar people; that ye should shew forth the praises of him who hath called you out of darkness into his marvellous light;"

Comfort
I find comfort in God's Word!

Psalm 23:4 - "Yea, though I walk through the valley of the shadow of death, I will fear no evil: for thou art with me; thy rod and thy staff they comfort me."

Psalm 46:1-3 - "God is our refuge and strength, a very present help in trouble. Therefore will not we fear, though the earth be removed, and though the mountains be carried into the midst of the sea; Though the waters thereof roar and be troubled, though the mountains shake with the swelling thereof. Selah."

Psalm 94:19 - "In the multitude of my thoughts within me thy comforts delight my soul."

Isaiah 49:13 - "Sing, O heavens; and be joyful, O earth; and break forth into singing, O mountains: for the LORD hath comforted his people, and will have mercy upon his afflicted."

John 6:37 - "All that the Father giveth me shall come to me; and him that cometh to me I will in no wise cast out."

Communication
My communication pleases the Lord!

Jeremiah 33:3 - "Call unto me, and I will answer thee, and shew thee great and mighty things, which thou knowest not."

Luke 24:15 - *"And it came to pass, that, while they communed together and reasoned, Jesus himself drew near, and went with them."*

1 Corinthians 15:33 - *"Be not deceived: evil communications corrupt good manners."*

Ephesians 4:29 - *"Let no corrupt communication proceed out of your mouth, but that which is good to the use of edifying, that it may minister grace unto the hearers."*

Colossians 3:8 - *"But now ye also put off all these; anger, wrath, malice, blasphemy, filthy communication out of your mouth."*

Philemon 1:6 - *"That the communication of thy faith may become effectual by the acknowledging of every good thing which is in you in Christ Jesus."*

Concerns

Every concern belongs to the Lord!

1 Kings 2:4 - *"If thy children take heed to their way, to walk before me in truth with all their heart and with all their soul, there shall not fail thee..."*

Psalm 94:11 - *"The LORD knoweth the thoughts of man, that they are vanity."*

Psalm 94:19 - *"In the multitude of my thoughts within me thy comforts delight my soul."*

Psalm 138:8 - *"The LORD will perfect that which concerneth me: thy mercy, O LORD, endureth for ever: forsake not the works of thine own hands."*

Ecclesiastes 1:13 - "And I gave my heart to seek and search out by wisdom concerning all things that are done under heaven: this sore travail hath God given to the sons of man to be exercised therewith."

1 Corinthians 12:1 - "Now concerning spiritual gifts, brethren, I would not have you ignorant."

1 Peter 5:7 - "Casting all your care upon him; for he careth for you."

Confession
I will profess the goodness of God!

Psalm 32:5 - "I acknowledge my sin unto thee, and mine iniquity have I not hid. I said, I will confess my transgressions unto the LORD; and thou forgavest the iniquity of my sin. Selah."

Proverbs 28:13 - "He that covereth his sins shall not prosper: but whoso confesseth and forsaketh them shall have mercy."

Matthew 10:32 - "Whosoever therefore shall confess me before men, him will I confess also before my Father which is in heaven."

Luke 12:8 - "Also I say unto you, Whosoever shall confess me before men, him shall the Son of man also confess before the angels of God:"

Romans 10:9 - "That if thou shalt confess with thy mouth the Lord Jesus, and shalt believe in thine heart that God hath raised him from the dead, thou shalt be saved."

Romans 10:10 - "For with the heart man believeth unto righteousness; and with the mouth confession is made unto salvation."

Confidence
My confidence is in God!

Psalm 55:22 - "Cast thy burden upon the LORD, and he shall sustain thee: he shall never suffer the righteous to be moved."

Proverbs 3:26 - "For the LORD shall be thy confidence, and shall keep thy foot from being taken."

2 Corinthians 5:6 - "Therefore we are always confident, knowing that, whilst we are at home in the body, we are absent from the Lord:"

Philippians 1:6 - "Being confident of this very thing, that he which hath begun a good work in you will perform it until the day of Jesus Christ:"

Hebrews 10:22 - "Let us draw near with a true heart in full assurance of faith, having our hearts sprinkled from an evil conscience, and our bodies washed with pure water."

1 John 3:20-21 - "For if our heart condemn us, God is greater than our heart, and knoweth all things. Beloved, if our heart condemn us not, then have we confidence toward God."

Contentment
I am content in the things of God!

Psalm 17:15 - "As for me, I will behold thy face in righteousness: I shall be satisfied, when I awake, with thy likeness."

Proverbs 19:23 - "The fear of the LORD tendeth to life: and he that hath it shall abide satisfied; he shall not be visited with evil."

Proverbs 21:19 - "It is better to dwell in the wilderness, than with a contentious and an angry woman."

Philippians 4:11 - "Not that I speak in respect of want: for I have learned, in whatsoever state I am, therewith to be content."

1 Timothy 6:6 - "But godliness with contentment is great gain."

1 Timothy 6:8 - "And having food and raiment let us be therewith content."

Hebrews 13:5 - "Let your conversation be without covetousness; and be content with such things as ye have: for he hath said, I will never leave thee, nor forsake thee."

Counsel
I will follow godly counsel!

Job 12:13 - "With him is wisdom and strength, he hath counsel and understanding."

Psalm 1:1 - "Blessed is the man that walketh not in the counsel of the ungodly, nor standeth in the way of sinners, nor sitteth in the seat of the scornful."

Psalm 13:2 - "How long shall I take counsel in my soul, having sorrow in my heart daily? how long shall mine enemy be exalted over me?"

Psalm 16:7 - "I will bless the LORD, who hath given me counsel: my reins also instruct me in the night seasons."

Psalm 73:24 - "Thou shalt guide me with thy counsel, and afterward receive me to glory. Thou shalt guide me with thy counsel, and afterward receive me to glory."

Proverbs 1:5 - "A wise man will hear, and will increase learning; and a man of understanding shall attain unto wise counsels:"

Proverbs 11:14 - "Where no counsel is, the people fall: but in the multitude of counsellors there is safety."

Covenant
My heart is in covenant relationship with God!

Genesis 17:2 - "And I will make my covenant between me and thee, and will multiply thee exceedingly."

Genesis 17:7 - "And I will establish my covenant between me and thee and thy seed after thee in their generations for an everlasting covenant, to be a God unto thee, and to thy seed after thee."

Exodus 31:3 - "And I have filled him with the spirit of God, in wisdom, and in understanding, and in knowledge, and in all manner of workmanship,"

Numbers 25:12 - "Wherefore say, Behold, I give unto him my covenant of peace:"

Deuteronomy 7:9 - "Know therefore that the LORD thy God, he is God, the faithful God, which keepeth covenant and mercy with them that love him and keep his commandments to a thousand generations;"

Mark 4:9 - "And he said unto them, He that hath ears to hear, let him hear."

Death

Death has no power over me!

Deuteronomy 30:15 - "See, I have set before thee this day life and good, and death and evil;"

Deuteronomy 30:19 - "I call heaven and earth to record this day against you, that I have set before you life and death, blessing and cursing: therefore choose life,"

Psalm 6:5 - "For in death there is no remembrance of thee: in the grave who shall give thee thanks?"

Psalm 9:13 - "Have mercy upon me, O LORD; consider my trouble which I suffer of them that hate me, thou that liftest me up from the gates of death:"

Psalm 23:4 - "Yea, though I walk through the valley of the shadow of death, I will fear no evil: for thou art with me; thy rod and thy staff they comfort me."

Psalm 116:8 - "For thou hast delivered my soul from death, mine eyes from tears, and my feet from falling."

Proverbs 14:12 - "There is a way which seemeth right unto a man, but the end thereof are the ways of death."

Deception

Deception will no longer have hold of me!

Deuteronomy 11:16 - "Take heed to yourselves, that your heart be not deceived, and ye turn aside, and serve other gods, and worship them;"

Job 15:31 - "Let not him that is deceived trust in vanity: for vanity shall be his recompence."

Proverbs 20:1 - "Wine is a mocker, strong drink is raging: and whosoever is deceived thereby is not wise."

Proverbs 24:28 - "Be not a witness against thy neighbour without cause; and deceive not with thy lips."

Jeremiah 9:5 - "And they will deceive every one his neighbour, and will not speak the truth: they have taught their tongue to speak lies, and weary themselves to commit iniquity."

Matthew 24:4 - "And Jesus answered and said unto them, Take heed that no man deceive you."

Mark 13:5 - "And Jesus answering them began to say, Take heed lest any man deceive you:"

Deliverance
When I call, He answers me!

Psalm 18:48 - "He delivereth me from mine enemies: yea, thou liftest me up above those that rise up against me: thou hast delivered me from the violent man."

Psalm 19:14 - "Let the words of my mouth, and the meditation of my heart, be acceptable in thy sight, O LORD, my strength, and my redeemer."

Psalm 32:7 - "Thou art my hiding place; thou shalt preserve me from trouble; thou shalt compass me about with songs of deliverance. Selah."

Psalm 34:4 - "I sought the LORD, and he heard me, and delivered me from all my fears."

Psalm 51:10 - "Create in me a clean heart, O God; and renew a right spirit within me."

Psalm 140:1 - "Deliver me, O LORD, from the evil man: preserve me from the violent man;"

Joel 2:32 - "And it shall come to pass, that whosoever shall call on the name of the LORD shall be delivered: for in mount Zion and in Jerusalem shall be deliverance, as the LORD hath said, and in the remnant whom the LORD shall call."

Luke 4:18 - "The Spirit of the Lord is upon me, because he hath anointed me to preach the gospel to the poor; he hath sent me to heal the brokenhearted, to preach deliverance to the captives, and recovering of sight to the blind, to set at liberty them that are bruised,"

Luke 9:29 - "And as he prayed, the fashion of his countenance was altered, and his raiment was white and glistering."

2 Timothy 3:11 - "Persecutions, afflictions, which came unto me at Antioch, at Iconium, at Lystra; what persecutions I endured: but out of them all the Lord delivered me."

2 Timothy 4:18 - "And the Lord shall deliver me from every evil work, and will preserve me unto his heavenly kingdom: to whom be glory for ever and ever. Amen."

Hebrews 4:15 - "For we have not an high priest which cannot be touched with the feeling of our infirmities; but was in all points tempted like as we are, yet without sin."

Encouragement
Today, I will encourage myself in the Word!

1 Samuel 30:6 - *"And David was greatly distressed; for the people spake of stoning him, because the soul of all the people was grieved, every man for his sons and for his daughters: but David encouraged himself in the LORD his God."*

2 Chronicles 35:2 - *"Thou art my hiding place; thou shalt preserve me from trouble; thou shalt compass me about with songs of deliverance. Selah."*

Ezra 10:4 - *"Arise; for this matter belongeth unto thee: we also will be with thee: be of good courage, and do it."*

Romans 14:19 - *"Let us therefore follow after the things which make for peace, and things wherewith one may edify another."*

Ephesians 5:19 - *"Speaking to yourselves in psalms and hymns and spiritual songs, singing and making melody in your heart to the Lord;"*

1 Thessalonians 5:11 - *"Wherefore comfort yourselves together, and edify one another, even as also ye do."*

Enemies
I am triumphant over my enemies!

Exodus 23:23 - *"For mine Angel shall go before thee, and bring thee in unto the Amorites, and the Hittites, and the Perizzites, and the Canaanites, the Hivites, and the Jebusites: and I will cut them off."*

2 Kings 17:39 - "But the LORD your God ye shall fear; and he shall deliver you out of the hand of all your enemies."

Psalm 5:8 - "Lead me, O LORD, in thy righteousness because of mine enemies; make thy way straight before my face."

Psalm 108:13 - "Through God we shall do valiantly: for he it is that shall tread down our enemies."

Matthew 5:44 - "But I say unto you, Love your enemies, bless them that curse you, do good to them that hate you, and pray for them which despitefully use you, and persecute you;"

1 Peter 5:8 - "Be sober, be vigilant; because your adversary the devil, as a roaring lion, walketh about, seeking whom he may devour:"

Envy
My bones shall rejoice in God!

Proverbs 3:31 - "Envy thou not the oppressor, and choose none of his ways."

Proverbs 14:30 - "A sound heart is the life of the flesh: but envy the rottenness of the bones."

Proverbs 23:17 - "Let not thine heart envy sinners: but be thou in the fear of the LORD all the day long."

Isaiah 26:11 - "LORD, when thy hand is lifted up, they will not see: but they shall see, and be ashamed for their envy at the people; yea, the fire of thine enemies shall devour them."

Romans 13:13 - "Let not thine heart envy sinners: but be thou in the fear of the LORD all the day long."

Galatians 5:26 - "Let us not be desirous of vain glory, provoking one another, envying one another."

James 3:16 - "For where envying and strife is, there is confusion and every evil work."

Everlasting Life
I am an Eternal Being through Christ!

Deuteronomy 30:19 - "I call heaven and earth to record this day against you, that I have set before you life and death, blessing and cursing: therefore choose life, that both thou and thy seed may live:"

Psalm 41:13 - "Blessed be the LORD God of Israel from everlasting, and to everlasting. Amen, and Amen."

Psalm 100:5 - "For the LORD is good; his mercy is everlasting; and his truth endureth to all generations."

Psalm 103:17 - "But the mercy of the LORD is from everlasting to everlasting upon them that fear him, and his righteousness unto children's children;"

Psalm 112:6 - "Surely he shall not be moved for ever: the righteous shall be in everlasting remembrance."

Proverbs 10:25 - "As the whirlwind passeth, so is the wicked no more: but the righteous is an everlasting foundation."

Matthew 7:14 - "Because strait is the gate, and narrow is the way, which leadeth unto life, and few there be that find it."

John 3:15 - "That whosoever believeth in him should not perish, but have eternal life."

John 3:36 - "He that believeth on the Son hath everlasting life: and he that believeth not the Son shall not see life; but the wrath of God abideth on him."

John 6:47 - "Verily, verily, I say unto you, He that believeth on me hath everlasting life."

Galatians 6:8 - "For he that soweth to his flesh shall of the flesh reap corruption; but he that soweth to the Spirit shall of the Spirit reap life everlasting."

Titus 3:5-7 - "Not by works of righteousness which we have done, but according to his mercy he saved us, by the washing of regeneration, and renewing of the Holy Ghost; Which he shed on us abundantly through Jesus Christ our Saviour; That being justified by his grace, we should be made heirs according to the hope of eternal life."

1 Timothy 1:16 - "Howbeit for this cause I obtained mercy, that in me first Jesus Christ might shew forth all longsuffering, for a pattern to them which should hereafter believe on him to life everlasting."

Evil
Goodness follows me!

Genesis 50:17 - "So shall ye say unto Joseph, Forgive, I pray thee now, the trespass of thy brethren, and their sin; for they did unto thee evil: and now, we pray thee, forgive the trespass of the servants of the God of thy father..."

Psalm 5:4 - "For thou art not a God that hath pleasure in wickedness: neither shall evil dwell with thee."

Psalm 34:13 - "Keep thy tongue from evil, and thy lips from speaking guile."

Psalm 37:9 - "For evildoers shall be cut off: but those that wait upon the LORD, they shall inherit the earth."

Proverbs 8:13 - "The fear of the LORD is to hate evil: pride, and arrogancy, and the evil way, and the froward mouth, do I hate."

Romans 12:21 - "Be not overcome of evil, but overcome evil with good."

1 Thessalonians 5:22 - "Abstain from all appearance of evil."

Exaltation
I will exalt my God forever!

Exodus 15:2 - "The LORD is my strength and song, and he is become my salvation: he is my God, and I will prepare him an habitation; my father's God, and I will exalt him."

2 Samuel 22:47 - "The LORD liveth; and blessed be my rock; and exalted be the God of the rock of my salvation."

Job 36:7 - "He withdraweth not his eyes from the righteous: but with kings are they on the throne; yea, he doth establish them for ever, and they are exalted."

Psalm 18:46 - "The LORD liveth; and blessed be my rock; and let the God of my salvation be exalted."

Psalm 34:3 - "O magnify the LORD with me, and let us exalt his name together."

Psalm 46:10 - "Be still, and know that I am God: I will be exalted among the heathen, I will be exalted in the earth."

1 Peter 5:6 - "Humble yourselves therefore under the mighty hand of God, that he may exalt you in due time:"

Faith
I walk by Faith!

Psalm 89:1 - "I will sing of the mercies of the LORD for ever: with my mouth will I make known thy faithfulness to all generations."

Proverbs 25:19 - "Confidence in an unfaithful man in time of trouble is like a broken tooth, and a foot out of joint."

Romans 4:17 - "(As it is written, I have made thee a father of many nations,) before him whom he believed, even God, who quickeneth the dead, and calleth those things which be not as though they were."

Hebrews 11:1 - "Now faith is the substance of things hoped for, the evidence of things not seen."

Hebrews 11:6 - "But without faith it is impossible to please him: for he that cometh to God must believe that he is, and that he is a rewarder of them that diligently seek him."

Revelation 21:4 - "And God shall wipe away all tears from their eyes; and there shall be no more death, neither sorrow, nor crying, neither shall there be any more pain: for the former things are passed away."

Faithful
I am a Faithful servant of God!

Deuteronomy 7:9 - "Know therefore that the LORD thy God, he is God, the faithful God, which keepeth covenant and mercy with them that love him and keep his commandments to a thousand generations;"

Psalm 31:23 - "O love the LORD, all ye his saints: for the LORD preserveth the faithful, and plentifully rewardeth the proud doer."

Psalm 36:5 - "Thy mercy, O LORD, is in the heavens; and thy faithfulness reacheth unto the clouds."

Psalm 119:11 - "Thy word have I hid in mine heart, that I might not sin against thee."

Proverbs 27:6 - "Faithful are the wounds of a friend; but the kisses of an enemy are deceitful."

Isaiah 25:1 - "O Lord, thou art my God; I will exalt thee, I will praise thy name; for thou hast done wonderful things; thy counsels of old are faithfulness and truth."

2 Thessalonians 3:3 - "But the Lord is faithful, who shall stablish you, and keep you from evil."

Faithfulness
I am filled with God's Faithfulness!

Psalm 89:1 - "I will sing of the mercies of the LORD for ever: with my mouth will I make known thy faithfulness to all generations."

Psalm 89:2 - "For I have said, Mercy shall be built up for ever: thy faithfulness shalt thou establish in the very heavens."

Psalm 89:33 - "Nevertheless my lovingkindness will I not utterly take from him, nor suffer my faithfulness to fail."

Proverbs 14:5 - "A faithful witness will not lie: but a false witness will utter lies."

Hosea 2:20 - "I will even betroth thee unto me in faithfulness: and thou shalt know the LORD."

Isaiah 11:5 - "And righteousness shall be the girdle of his loins, and faithfulness the girdle of his reins."

Lamentations 3:23 - "They are new every morning: great is thy faithfulness."

Favor

The Favor of God dwells with me!

Ruth 1:8 - "And Naomi said unto her two daughters in law, Go, return each to her mother's house: the LORD deal kindly with you, as ye have dealt with the dead, and with me."

Ruth 2:13 - "Then she said, Let me find favour in thy sight, my lord; for that thou hast comforted me, and for that thou hast spoken friendly unto thine handmaid, though I be not like unto one of thine handmaidens."

1 Samuel 20:14 - "And thou shalt not only while yet I live shew me the kindness of the LORD, that I die not:"

Proverbs 12:2 - "A good man obtaineth favour of the LORD: but a man of wicked devices will he condemn."

Proverbs 16:22 - "Understanding is a wellspring of life unto him that hath it: but the instruction of fools is folly."

Micah 7:18 - "Who is a God like unto thee, that pardoneth iniquity, and passeth by the transgression of the remnant of his heritage? he retaineth not his anger for ever, because he delighteth in mercy."

Fear
I refuse to live in fear!

Deuteronomy 10:20 - "Thou shalt fear the LORD thy God; him shalt thou serve, and to him shalt thou cleave, and swear by his name."

2 Kings 17:38 - "And the covenant that I have made with you ye shall not forget; neither shall ye fear other gods."

Psalm 27:1 - "The LORD is my light and my salvation; whom shall I fear? the LORD is the strength of my life; of whom shall I be afraid?"

Psalm 91:5 - "Thou shalt not be afraid for the terror by night; nor for the arrow that flieth by day;"

Isaiah 41:10 - "Fear thou not; for I am with thee: be not dismayed; for I am thy God: I will strengthen thee; yea, I will help thee; yea, I will uphold thee with the right hand of my righteousness."

Romans 8:15 - "For ye have not received the spirit of bondage again to fear; but ye have received the Spirit of adoption, whereby we cry, Abba, Father."

Fear of God

Godly fear keeps me on the narrow path!

Deuteronomy 1:21 - *"Behold, the LORD thy God hath set the land before thee: go up and possess it, as the LORD God of thy fathers hath said unto thee; fear not, neither be discouraged."*

Deuteronomy 6:2 - *"That thou mightest fear the LORD thy God, to keep all his statutes and his commandments, which I command thee, thou, and thy son, and thy son's son, all the days of thy life; and that thy days may be prolonged."*

1 Samuel 12:14 - *"If ye will fear the LORD, and serve him, and obey his voice, and not rebel against the commandment of the LORD, then shall both ye and also the king that reigneth over you continue following the LORD your God:"*

2 Kings 17:39 - *"But the LORD your God ye shall fear; and he shall deliver you out of the hand of all your enemies."*

1 Chronicles 16:25 - *"For great is the LORD, and greatly to be praised: he also is to be feared above all gods."*

Luke 1:50 - *"And his mercy is on them that fear him from generation to generation."*

Focus
My focus is on the things of God!

1 Samuel 16:7 - "But the LORD said unto Samuel, Look not on his countenance, or on the height of his stature; because I have refused him: for the LORD seeth not as man seeth; for man looketh on the outward appearance, but the LORD looketh on the heart."

Proverbs 4:25 - "Let thine eyes look right on, and let thine eyelids look straight before thee."

Isaiah 43:7 - "Even every one that is called by my name: for I have created him for my glory, I have formed him; yea, I have made him."

Luke 9:62 - "And Jesus said unto him, No man, having put his hand to the plough, and looking back, is fit for the kingdom of God."

John 7:24 - "Judge not according to the appearance, but judge righteous judgment."

Galatians 4:19 - "My little children, of whom I travail in birth again until Christ be formed in you,"

Forgiveness
I choose to forgive and be forgiven!

2 Chronicles 7:14 - "If my people, which are called by my name, shall humble themselves, and pray, and seek my face, and turn from their wicked ways; then will I hear from heaven, and will forgive their sin, and will heal their land."

Daniel 9:9 - "To the Lord our God belong mercies and forgivenesses, though we have rebelled against him;"

Psalm 25:18 - "Look upon mine affliction and my pain; and forgive all my sins."

Psalm 32:1 - "Blessed is he whose transgression is forgiven, whose sin is covered."

Psalm 86:5 - "For thou, Lord, art good, and ready to forgive; and plenteous in mercy unto all them that call upon thee."

Psalm 103:12 - "As far as the east is from the west, so far hath he removed our transgressions from us."

Psalm 130:4 - "But there is forgiveness with thee, that thou mayest be feared."

Matthew 6:14-15 - "For if ye forgive men their trespasses, your heavenly Father will also forgive you: But if ye forgive not men their trespasses, neither will your Father forgive your trespasses."

Matthew 12:31 - "Wherefore I say unto you, All manner of sin and blasphemy shall be forgiven unto men: but the blasphemy against the Holy Ghost shall not be forgiven unto men."

Mark 11:25 - "And when ye stand praying, forgive, if ye have ought against any: that your Father also which is in heaven may forgive you your trespasses."

Luke 6:37 - "Judge not, and ye shall not be judged: condemn not, and ye shall not be condemned: forgive, and ye shall be forgiven:"

Luke 23:34 - "Then said Jesus, Father, forgive them; for they know not what they do. And they parted his raiment, and cast lots."

Ephesians 4:32 - "And be ye kind one to another, tenderhearted, forgiving one another, even as God for Christ's sake hath forgiven you."

Freedom

Through repentance, I live in freedom!

Psalm 51:12 - "Restore unto me the joy of thy salvation; and uphold me with thy free spirit."

Ecclesiastes 5:20 - "For he shall not much remember the days of his life; because God answereth him in the joy of his heart."

John 8:32 - "And ye shall know the truth, and the truth shall make you free."

John 8:36 - "If the Son therefore shall make you free, ye shall be free indeed."

Romans 3:24 - "Being justified freely by his grace through the redemption that is in Christ Jesus:"

Romans 5:15 - "But not as the offence, so also is the free gift. For if through the offence of one many be dead, much more the grace of God, and the gift by grace, which is by one man, Jesus Christ, hath abounded unto many."

Romans 6:18 - "Being then made free from sin, ye became the servants of righteousness."

Romans 6:22 - "But now being made free from sin, and become servants to God, ye have your fruit unto holiness, and the end everlasting life."

Romans 8:1-2 - "There is therefore now no condemnation to them which are in Christ Jesus, who walk not after the flesh, but after the Spirit. For the law of the Spirit of life in Christ Jesus hath made me free from the law of sin and death."

2 Corinthians 3:17 - "Now the Lord is that Spirit: and where the Spirit of the Lord is, there is liberty."

2 Corinthians 5:17 - "Therefore if any man be in Christ, he is a new creature: old things are passed away; behold, all things are become new."

Galatians 5:1 - "Stand fast therefore in the liberty wherewith Christ hath made us free, and be not entangled again with the yoke of bondage."

Revelation 22:17 - "And the Spirit and the bride say, Come. And let him that heareth say, Come. And let him that is athirst come. And whosoever will, let him take the water of life freely."

Fruit of the Spirit
Christ in me shall produce good fruit!

Psalm 1:3 - "And he shall be like a tree planted by the rivers of water, that bringeth forth his fruit in his season; his leaf also shall not wither; and whatsoever he doeth shall prosper."

Proverbs 11:30 - "The fruit of the righteous is a tree of life; and he that winneth souls is wise."

Matthew 7:17 - "Even so every good tree bringeth forth good fruit; but a corrupt tree bringeth forth evil fruit."

Luke 6:43 - "For a good tree bringeth not forth corrupt fruit; neither doth a corrupt tree bring forth good fruit."

Romans 8:23 - "And not only they, but ourselves also, which have the firstfruits of the Spirit,"

Galatians 5:22-23 - "But the fruit of the Spirit is love, joy, peace, longsuffering, gentleness, goodness, faith, Meekness, temperance: against such there is no law."

Ephesians 5:9 - "(For the fruit of the Spirit is in all goodness and righteousness and truth;)"

Gifts
Christ is the gift who lives inside me!

Proverbs 15:27 - "He that is greedy of gain troubleth his own house; but he that hateth gifts shall live."

Matthew 7:11 - "If ye then, being evil, know how to give good gifts unto your children, how much more shall your Father which is in heaven give good things to them that ask him?"

Luke 11:13 - "If ye then, being evil, know how to give good gifts unto your children: how much more shall your heavenly Father give the Holy Spirit to them that ask him?"

Romans 11:29 - "For the gifts and calling of God are without repentance."

1 Corinthians 14:1 - "Follow after charity, and desire spiritual gifts, but rather that ye may prophesy."

James 1:17 - "Every good gift and every perfect gift is from above, and cometh down from the Father of lights, with whom is no variableness, neither shadow of turning."

Giving
I am blessed to give!

Psalm 69:30 - "I will praise the name of God with a song, and will magnify him with thanksgiving."

Psalm 100:4 - "Enter into his gates with thanksgiving, and into his courts with praise: be thankful unto him, and bless his name."

Luke 6:38 - "Give, and it shall be given unto you; good measure, pressed down, and shaken together, and running over, shall men give into your bosom. For with the same measure that ye mete withal it shall be measured to you again."

Acts 20:35 - "I have shewed you all things, how that so labouring ye ought to support the weak, and to remember the words of the Lord Jesus, how he said, It is more blessed to give than to receive."

Ephesians 5:20 - "Giving thanks always for all things unto God and the Father in the name of our Lord Jesus Christ;"

1 Peter 3:7 - "Likewise, ye husbands, dwell with them according to knowledge, giving honour unto the wife, as unto the weaker vessel, and as being heirs together of the grace of life; that your prayers be not hindered."

God
Almighty God, Prince of Peace!

Genesis 1:31 - "And God saw every thing that he had made, and, behold, it was very good..."

Exodus 20:3 - "Thou shalt have no other gods before me."

Exodus 20:5 - "Thou shalt not bow down thyself to them, nor serve them: for I the LORD thy God am a jealous God, visiting the iniquity of the fathers upon the children unto the third and fourth generation of them that hate me;"

Exodus 29:45 - "And I will dwell among the children of Israel, and will be their God."

Exodus 31:3 - "And I have filled him with the spirit of God, in wisdom, and in understanding, and in knowledge, and in all manner of workmanship,"

Deuteronomy 32:35 - "To me belongeth vengeance and recompence; their foot shall slide in due time: for the day of their calamity is at hand, and the things that shall come upon them make haste."

1 Samuel 17:45 - "Then said David to the Philistine, Thou comest to me with a sword, and with a spear, and with a shield: but I come to thee in the name of the LORD of hosts, the God of the armies of Israel, whom thou hast defied."

Psalm 135:5 - "For I know that the LORD is great, and that our Lord is above all gods."

Isaiah 9:6 - "For unto us a child is born, unto us a son is given: and the government shall be upon his shoulder: and his name shall be called Wonderful, Counsellor, The mighty God, The everlasting Father, The Prince of Peace."

Jeremiah 32:17 - "Ah Lord GOD! behold, thou hast made the heaven and the earth by thy great power and stretched out arm, and there is nothing too hard for thee:"

Nahum 1:2 - "God is jealous, and the LORD revengeth; the LORD revengeth, and is furious; the LORD will take vengeance on his adversaries, and he reserveth wrath for his enemies."

John 3:30 - "He must increase, but I must decrease."

2 Corinthians 4:7 - "But we have this treasure in earthen vessels, that the excellency of the power may be of God, and not of us."

God Pleaser
I choose to be a God pleaser!

Leviticus 11:45 - "For I am the LORD that bringeth you up out of the land of Egypt, to be your God: ye shall therefore be holy, for I am holy."

Ephesians 6:6 - "Not with eyeservice, as menpleasers; but as the servants of Christ, doing the will of God from the heart;"

Colossians 3:22 - "Servants, obey in all things your masters according to the flesh; not with eyeservice, as menpleasers; but in singleness of heart, fearing God;"

1 Thessalonians 2:4 - "But as we were allowed of God to be put in trust with the gospel, even so we speak; not as pleasing men, but God, which trieth our hearts."

1 Timothy 4:12 - "Let no man despise thy youth; but be thou an example of the believers, in word, in conversation, in charity, in spirit, in faith, in purity."

1 John 3:22 - "And whatsoever we ask, we receive of him, because we keep his commandments, and do those things that are pleasing in his sight."

Godly Order
He orders my steps!

Psalm 50:23 - "Whoso offereth praise glorifieth me: and to him that ordereth his conversation aright will I shew the salvation of God."

Psalm 119:33 - "Order my steps in thy word: and let not any iniquity have dominion over me."

1 Corinthians 14:40 - "Let all things be done decently and in order."

2 Thessalonians 3:6 - "Now we command you, brethren, in the name of our Lord Jesus Christ, that ye withdraw yourselves from every brother that walketh disorderly, and not after the tradition which he received of us."

Hebrews 6:20 - "Whither the forerunner is for us entered, even Jesus, made an high priest for ever after the order of Melchisedec."

Hebrews 12:28 - "Wherefore we receiving a kingdom which cannot be moved, let us have grace, whereby we may serve God acceptably with reverence and godly fear:"

Grace
Saved by Grace!

Exodus 33:17 - "And the LORD said unto Moses, I will do this thing also that thou hast spoken: for thou hast found grace in my sight, and I know thee by name."

Ruth 2:10 - "Then she fell on her face, and bowed herself to the ground, and said unto him, Why have I found grace in thine eyes, that thou shouldest take knowledge of me, seeing I am a stranger?"

Psalm 84:11 - "For the LORD God is a sun and shield: the LORD will give grace and glory: no good thing will he withhold from them that walk uprightly."

Proverbs 1:9 - "For they shall be an ornament of grace unto thy head, and chains about thy neck."

Hebrews 4:16 - "Let us therefore come boldly unto the throne of grace, that we may obtain mercy, and find grace to help in time of need."

2 Peter 3:18 - "But grow in grace, and in the knowledge of our Lord and Saviour Jesus Christ. To him be glory both now and for ever. Amen."

Guidance
The Holy Spirit guides my steps!

Deuteronomy 31:8 - "And the LORD, he it is that doth go before thee; he will be with thee, he will not fail thee, neither forsake thee: fear not, neither be dismayed."

Psalm 31:3 - "For thou art my rock and my fortress; therefore for thy name's sake lead me, and guide me."

Psalm 32:8 - "I will instruct thee and teach thee in the way which thou shalt go: I will guide thee with mine eye."

Psalm 73:24 - "Thou shalt guide me with thy counsel, and afterward receive me to glory."

Psalm 119:105 - "Thy word is a lamp unto my feet, and a light unto my path."

Romans 2:19 - "And art confident that thou thyself art a guide of the blind, a light of them which are in darkness,"

2 Thessalonians 3:5 - "And the Lord direct your hearts into the love of God, and into the patient waiting for Christ."

Happiness
Happiness is a choice!

1 Kings 10:8 - "Happy are thy men, happy are these thy servants, which stand continually before thee, and that hear thy wisdom."

Psalm 31:7 - "I will be glad and rejoice in thy mercy: for thou hast considered my trouble; thou hast known my soul in adversities;"

Psalm 37:4 - "Delight thyself also in the LORD: and he shall give thee the desires of thine heart."

Proverbs 29:18 - "Where there is no vision, the people perish: but he that keepeth the law, happy is he."

Isaiah 58:14 - "Then shalt thou delight thyself in the LORD; and I will cause thee to ride upon the high places of the earth, and feed thee with the heritage of Jacob thy father: for the mouth of the LORD hath spoken it."

1 Peter 3:14 - "But and if ye suffer for righteousness' sake, happy are ye: and be not afraid of their terror, neither be troubled;"

Harmony
I am in Harmony with Creation!

Amos 3:3 - "Can two walk together, except they be agreed?"

2 Corinthians 6:16 - "And what agreement hath the temple of God with idols? for ye are the temple of the living God; as God hath said, I will dwell in them, and walk in them; and I will be their God, and they shall be my people."

Matthew 18:20 - "For where two or three are gathered together in my name, there am I in the midst of them."

1 John 5:7 - "For there are three that bear record in heaven, the Father, the Word, and the Holy Ghost: and these three are one."

1 John 5:8 - "And there are three that bear witness in earth, the Spirit, and the water, and the blood: and these three agree in one."

Revelation 17:17 - "For God hath put in their hearts to fulfil his will, and to agree, and give their kingdom unto the beast, until the words of God shall be fulfilled."

Hatred
I choose to love!

2 Samuel 22:18 - "He delivered me from my strong enemy, and from them that hated me: for they were too strong for me."

Psalm 94:1 - "O Lord God, to whom vengeance belongeth; O God, to whom vengeance belongeth, shew thyself."

Psalm 97:10 - "Ye that love the LORD, hate evil: he preserveth the souls of his saints; he delivereth them out of the hand of the wicked."

Psalm 139:22 - "I hate them with perfect hatred: I count them mine enemies."

Proverbs 10:12 - "Hatred stirreth up strifes: but love covereth all sins."

Proverbs 10:18 - "He that hideth hatred with lying lips, and he that uttereth a slander, is a fool."

Proverbs 26:26 - "Whose hatred is covered by deceit, his wickedness shall be shewed before the whole congregation."

Healing
With His stripes, I am healed!

2 Kings 20:5 - "Turn again, and tell Hezekiah the captain of my people, Thus saith the LORD, the God of David thy father, I have heard thy prayer, I have seen thy tears: behold, I will heal thee: on the third day thou shalt go up unto the house of the LORD."

Psalm 103:2-3 - "Bless the LORD, O my soul, and forget not all his benefits: Who forgiveth all thine iniquities; who healeth all thy diseases;"

Psalm 147:3 - "He healeth the broken in heart, and bindeth up their wounds."

Isaiah 53:5 - "But he was wounded for our transgressions, he was bruised for our iniquities: the chastisement of our peace was upon him; and with his stripes we are healed."

Malachi 4:2 - *"But unto you that fear my name shall the Sun of righteousness arise with healing in his wings;"*

Matthew 4:23 - *"And Jesus went about all Galilee, teaching in their synagogues, and preaching the gospel of the kingdom, and healing all manner of sickness and all manner of disease among the people."*

Matthew 9:12 - *"But when Jesus heard that, he said unto them, They that be whole need not a physician, but they that are sick."*

Mark 2:17 - *"When Jesus heard it, he saith unto them, They that are whole have no need of the physician, but they that are sick: I came not to call the righteous, but sinners to repentance."*

Acts 10:38 - *"How God anointed Jesus of Nazareth with the Holy Ghost and with power: who went about doing good, and healing all that were oppressed of the devil; for God was with him."*

Romans 8:26 - *"Likewise the Spirit also helpeth our infirmities: for we know not what we should pray for as we ought: but the Spirit itself maketh intercession for us with groanings which cannot be uttered."*

Colossians 4:12 - *"Epaphras, who is one of you, a servant of Christ, saluteth you, always labouring fervently for you in prayers, that ye may stand perfect and complete in all the will of God."*

1 Peter 2:24 - *"Who his own self bare our sins in his own body on the tree, that we, being dead to sins, should live unto righteousness: by whose stripes ye were healed."*

Health
I walk in divine health!

Genesis 1:29-30 - "And God said, Behold, I have given you every herb bearing seed, which is upon the face of all the earth, and every tree, in the which is the fruit of a tree yielding seed; to you it shall be for meat. And to every beast of the earth, and to every fowl of the air, and to every thing that creepeth upon the earth, wherein there is life, I have given every green herb for meat: and it was so."

Psalm 42:11 - "Why art thou cast down, O my soul? and why art thou disquieted within me? hope thou in God: for I shall yet praise him, who is the health of my countenance, and my God."

Proverbs 3:8 - "It shall be health to thy navel, and marrow to thy bones."

Proverbs 4:20 - "My son, attend to my words; incline thine ear unto my sayings."

Proverbs 4:22 - "For they are life unto those that find them, and health to all their flesh."

Proverbs 16:24 - "Pleasant words are as an honeycomb, sweet to the soul, and health to the bones."

Proverbs 17:22 - "A merry heart doeth good like a medicine: but a broken spirit drieth the bones."

Isaiah 58:8 - "Then shall thy light break forth as the morning, and thine health shall spring forth speedily: and thy righteousness shall go before thee; the glory of the LORD shall be thy rereward."

Jeremiah 30:17 - "For I will restore health unto thee, and I will heal thee of thy wounds, saith the LORD;"

Ezekiel 47:12 - *"And by the river upon the bank thereof, on this side and on that side, shall grow all trees for meat, whose leaf shall not fade, neither shall the fruit thereof be consumed: it shall bring forth new fruit according to his months, because their waters they issued out of the sanctuary: and the fruit thereof shall be for meat, and the leaf thereof for medicine."*

3 John 1:2 - *"Beloved, I wish above all things that thou mayest prosper and be in health, even as thy soul prospereth."*

Revelation 2:7 - *"He that hath an ear, let him hear what the Spirit saith unto the churches; To him that overcometh will I give to eat of the tree of life, which is in the midst of the paradise of God."*

Heart

My heart rejoices in the God of my Salvation!

Leviticus 19:17 - *"Thou shalt not hate thy brother in thine heart: thou shalt in any wise rebuke thy neighbour, and not suffer sin upon him."*

Deuteronomy 4:39 - *"Know therefore this day, and consider it in thine heart, that the LORD he is God in heaven above, and upon the earth beneath: there is none else."*

Deuteronomy 6:5 - *"And thou shalt love the LORD thy God with all thine heart, and with all thy soul, and with all thy might."*

Deuteronomy 11:16 - *"Take heed to yourselves, that your heart be not deceived, and ye turn aside, and serve other gods, and worship them;"*

Psalm 33:21 - *"For our heart shall rejoice in him, because we have trusted in his holy name."*

Proverbs 4:23 - *"Keep thy heart with all diligence; for out of it are the issues of life."*

Proverbs 15:13 - *"A merry heart maketh a cheerful countenance: but by sorrow of the heart the spirit is broken."*

Ecclesiastes 7:3 - *"Sorrow is better than laughter: for by the sadness of the countenance the heart is made better."*

Ecclesiastes 7:22 - *"For oftentimes also thine own heart knoweth that thou thyself likewise hast cursed others."*

Matthew 12:34-35 - *"O generation of vipers, how can ye, being evil, speak good things? for out of the abundance of the heart the mouth speaketh. A good man out of the good treasure of the heart bringeth forth good things: and an evil man out of the evil treasure bringeth forth evil things."*

Matthew 8:35 - *"So likewise shall my heavenly Father do also unto you, if ye from your hearts forgive not every one his brother their trespasses."*

Mark 7:18-20 - *"And he saith unto them, Are ye so without understanding also? Do ye not perceive, that whatsoever thing from without entereth into the man, it cannot defile him; Because it entereth not into his heart, but into the belly, and goeth out into the draught, purging all meats? And he said, That which cometh out of the man, that defileth the man."*

Luke 12:34 - *"For where your treasure is, there will your heart be also."*

Heaven

Heaven is the space surrounding Earth!

Deuteronomy 4:36 - "Out of heaven he made thee to hear his voice, that he might instruct thee: and upon earth he shewed thee his great fire; and thou heardest his words out of the midst of the fire."

Deuteronomy 32:40 - "For I lift up my hand to heaven, and say, I live for ever."

1 Chronicles 16:31 - "Let the heavens be glad, and let the earth rejoice: and let men say among the nations, The LORD reigneth."

1 Chronicles 29:11 - "Thine, O LORD is the greatness, and the power, and the glory, and the victory, and the majesty: for all that is in the heaven and in the earth is thine; thine is the kingdom, O LORD, and thou art exalted as head above all."

2 Chronicles 7:14 - "If my people, which are called by my name, shall humble themselves, and pray, and seek my face, and turn from their wicked ways; then will I hear from heaven, and will forgive their sin, and will heal their land."

Nehemiah 9:15 - "And gavest them bread from heaven for their hunger, and broughtest forth water for them out of the rock for their thirst, and promisedst them that they should go in to possess the land which thou hadst sworn to give them."

Psalm 108:4 - "For thy mercy is great above the heavens: and thy truth reacheth unto the clouds."

Psalm 115:15 - "Ye are blessed of the LORD which made heaven and earth."

Matthew 5:16 - *"Let your light so shine before men, that they may see your good works, and glorify your Father which is in heaven."*

Matthew 16:19 - *"And I will give unto thee the keys of the kingdom of heaven: and whatsoever thou shalt bind on earth shall be bound in heaven: and whatsoever thou shalt loose on earth shall be loosed in heaven."*

Matthew 24:35 - *"Heaven and earth shall pass away, but my words shall not pass away."*

Romans 8:24 - *"For we are saved by hope: but hope that is seen is not hope: for what a man seeth, why doth he yet hope for?"*

Holiness

Holiness dwells in me!

Genesis 2:24 - *"Therefore shall a man leave his father and his mother, and shall cleave unto his wife: and they shall be one flesh."*

Psalm 96:9 - *"O worship the LORD in the beauty of holiness: fear before him, all the earth."*

Romans 6:22 - *"But now being made free from sin, and become servants to God, ye have your fruit unto holiness, and the end everlasting life."*

2 Corinthians 7:1 - *"Having therefore these promises, dearly beloved, let us cleanse ourselves from all filthiness of the flesh and spirit, perfecting holiness in the fear of God."*

Ephesians 1:4 - *"According as he hath chosen us in him before the foundation of the world, that we should be holy and without blame before him in love:"*

1 Peter 1:15 - "But as he which hath called you is holy, so be ye holy in all manner of conversation;"

Holy Spirit
The Holy Spirit is alive in me!

Psalm 51:11 - "Cast me not away from thy presence; and take not thy holy spirit from me."

Luke 11:13 - "If ye then, being evil, know how to give good gifts unto your children: how much more shall your heavenly Father give the Holy Spirit to them that ask him?"

Acts 1:8 - "But ye shall receive power, after that the Holy Ghost is come upon you: and ye shall be witnesses unto me both in Jerusalem, and in all Judaea, and in Samaria, and unto the uttermost part of the earth."

Acts 2:4 - "And they were all filled with the Holy Ghost, and began to speak with other tongues, as the Spirit gave them utterance."

Romans 8:9-10 - "And if Christ be in you, the body is dead because of sin; but the Spirit is life because of righteousness. And if Christ be in you, the body is dead because of sin; but the Spirit is life because of righteousness."

1 Thessalonians 4:8 - "He therefore that despiseth, despiseth not man, but God, who hath also given unto us his holy Spirit."

Honor
I am a vessel of Honor!

Deuteronomy 5:16 - "Honour thy father and thy mother, as the LORD thy God hath commanded thee; that thy days may be prolonged, and that it may go well with thee, in the land which the LORD thy God giveth thee."

1 Chronicles 16:27 - "Glory and honour are in his presence; strength and gladness are in his place."

1 Chronicles 29:12 - "Both riches and honour come of thee, and thou reignest over all; and in thine hand is power and might; and in thine hand it is to make great, and to give strength unto all."

2 Chronicles 1:11-12 - "And God said to Solomon, Because this was in thine heart, and thou hast not asked riches, wealth, or honour, nor the life of thine enemies, neither yet hast asked long life; but hast asked wisdom and knowledge for thyself, that thou mayest judge my people, over whom I have made thee king: Wisdom and knowledge is granted unto thee; and I will give thee riches, and wealth, and honour, such as none of the kings have had that have been before thee, neither shall there any after thee have the like."

Psalm 71:8 - "Let my mouth be filled with thy praise and with thy honour all the day."

Psalm 91:15 - "He shall call upon me, and I will answer him: I will be with him in trouble; I will deliver him, and honour him."

Proverbs 3:9 - "Honour the LORD with thy substance, and with the firstfruits of all thine increase:"

Proverbs 13:18 - "Poverty and shame shall be to him that refuseth instruction: but he that regardeth reproof shall be honoured."

Proverbs 21:21 - "He that followeth after righteousness and mercy findeth life, righteousness, and honour."

Proverbs 22:4 - "By humility and the fear of the LORD are riches, and honour, and life."

2 Timothy 2:21 - "If a man therefore purge himself from these, he shall be a vessel unto honour, sanctified, and meet for the master's use, and prepared unto every good work."

1 Peter 2:17 - "Honour all men. Love the brotherhood. Fear God. Honour the king."

Hope
My hope is in God!

Job 14:7 - "For there is hope of a tree, if it be cut down, that it will sprout again, and that the tender branch thereof will not cease."

Psalm 16:9 - "Therefore my heart is glad, and my glory rejoiceth: my flesh also shall rest in hope."

Psalm 31:24 - "Be of good courage, and he shall strengthen your heart, all ye that hope in the LORD."

Psalm 33:18 - "Behold, the eye of the LORD is upon them that fear him, upon them that hope in his mercy;"

Psalm 33:20 - "Our soul waiteth for the LORD: he is our help and our shield."

Psalm 38:15 - "For in thee, O LORD, do I hope: thou wilt hear, O Lord my God."

Psalm 43:5 - "Why art thou cast down, O my soul? and why art thou disquieted within me? hope in God: for I shall yet praise him, who is the health of my countenance, and my God."

Psalm 71:14 - "But I will hope continually, and will yet praise thee more and more."

Psalm 78:7 - "That they might set their hope in God, and not forget the works of God, but keep his commandments:"

Psalm 119:81 - "My soul fainteth for thy salvation: but I hope in thy word."

Psalm 119:114 - "Thou art my hiding place and my shield: I hope in thy word."

Psalm 121:1 - "I will lift up mine eyes unto the hills, from whence cometh my help."

Psalm 130:5 - "I wait for the LORD, my soul doth wait, and in his word do I hope."

Psalm 146:5 - "Happy is he that hath the God of Jacob for his help, whose hope is in the LORD his God:"

1 John 3:2-3 - "Beloved, now are we the sons of God, and it doth not yet appear what we shall be: but we know that, when he shall appear, we shall be like him; for we shall see him as he is. And every man that hath this hope in him purifieth himself, even as he is pure."

Human Form
I am created in God's own image!

Genesis 1:27 - "So God created man in his own image, in the image of God created he him; male and female created he them."

James 4:14 - "Whereas ye know not what shall be on the morrow. For what is your life? It is even a vapour, that appeareth for a little time, and then vanisheth away."

Humility
I am clothed in humility!

Psalm 139:23 - "Search me, O God, and know my heart: try me, and know my thoughts:"

Proverbs 15:33 - "The fear of the LORD is the instruction of wisdom; and before honour is humility."

Proverbs 18:12 - "Before destruction the heart of man is haughty, and before honour is humility."

Proverbs 22:4 - "By humility and the fear of the LORD are riches, and honour, and life."

Acts 20:19 - "Serving the LORD with all humility of mind, and with many tears, and temptations,"

Colossians 2:23 - "Which things have indeed a shew of wisdom in will worship, and humility, and neglecting of the body: not in any honour to the satisfying of the flesh."

1 Peter 5:5 - "Likewise, ye younger, submit yourselves unto the elder. Yea, all of you be subject one to another, and be clothed with humility: for God resisteth the proud, and giveth grace to the humble."

𝒥nheritance

I choose to receive my Kingdom Inheritance!

Psalm 16:5 - "The LORD is the portion of mine inheritance and of my cup..."

Psalm 33:12 - "Blessed is the nation whose God is the LORD; and the people whom he hath chosen for his own inheritance."

Psalm 37:18 - "The LORD knoweth the days of the upright: and their inheritance shall be for ever."

Psalm 94:14 - "For the LORD will not cast off his people, neither will he forsake his inheritance."

Proverbs 8:21 - "That I may cause those that love me to inherit substance; and I will fill their treasures."

Acts 26:18 - "To open their eyes, and to turn them from darkness to light, and from the power of Satan unto God, that they may receive forgiveness of sins, and inheritance among them which are sanctified by faith that is in me."

Ephesians 1:14 - "Which is the earnest of our inheritance until the redemption of the purchased possession, unto the praise of his glory."

Intercession
Jesus is my Intercessor!

Isaiah 59:16 - "And he saw that there was no man, and wondered that there was no intercessor: therefore his arm brought salvation unto him; and his righteousness, it sustained him."

Romans 8:26 - "Likewise the Spirit also helpeth our infirmities: for we know not what we should pray for as we ought: but the Spirit itself maketh intercession for us with groanings which cannot be uttered."

Romans 8:27 - "And he that searcheth the hearts knoweth what is the mind of the Spirit, because he maketh intercession for the saints according to the will of God."

Romans 8:34 - "Who is he that condemneth? It is Christ that died, yea rather, that is risen again, who is even at the right hand of God, who also maketh intercession for us."

1 Timothy 2:5 - "For there is one God, and one mediator between God and men, the man Christ Jesus;"

Hebrews 7:25 - "Wherefore he is able also to save them to the uttermost that come unto God by him, seeing he ever liveth to make intercession for them."

Jealousy
I am created perfectly in God!

Deuteronomy 4:24 - "For the LORD thy God is a consuming fire, even a jealous God."

Proverbs 6:34 - "For jealousy is the rage of a man: therefore he will not spare in the day of vengeance."

Song of Solomon 8:6 - "Set me as a seal upon thine heart, as a seal upon thine arm: for love is strong as death; jealousy is cruel as the grave: the coals thereof are coals of fire, which hath a most vehement flame."

Nahum 1:2 - "God is jealous, and the LORD revengeth; the LORD revengeth, and is furious; the LORD will take vengeance on his adversaries, and he reserveth wrath for his enemies."

Zephaniah 3:8 - "Therefore wait ye upon me, saith the LORD, until the day that I rise up to the prey: ...that I may assemble the kingdoms, to pour upon them mine indignation, even all my fierce anger: for all the earth shall be devoured with the fire of my jealousy."

2 Corinthians 11:2 - "For I am jealous over you with godly jealousy: for I have espoused you to one husband, that I may present you as a chaste virgin to Christ."

Joy
Joy fills my soul!

Job 33:26 - "He shall pray unto God, and he will be favourable unto him: and he shall see his face with joy: for he will render unto man his righteousness."

Psalm 5:11 - "But let all those that put their trust in thee rejoice: let them ever shout for joy, because thou defendest them: let them also that love thy name be joyful in thee."

Psalm 16:11 - "Thou wilt shew me the path of life: in thy presence is fulness of joy; at thy right hand there are pleasures for evermore."

Psalm 30:5 - "For his anger endureth but a moment; in his favour is life: weeping may endure for a night, but joy cometh in the morning."

Psalm 30:11 - "Thou hast turned for me my mourning into dancing: thou hast put off my sackcloth, and girded me with gladness;"

Psalm 32:11 - "Be glad in the LORD, and rejoice, ye righteous: and shout for joy, all ye that are upright in heart."

Psalm 126:5-6 - "They that sow in tears shall reap in joy. He that goeth forth and weepeth, bearing precious seed, shall doubtless come again with rejoicing, bringing his sheaves with him."

Ecclesiastes 2:26 - "For God giveth to a man that is good in his sight wisdom, and knowledge, and joy..."

Ecclesiastes 5:20 - "For he shall not much remember the days of his life; because God answereth him in the joy of his heart."

Isaiah 12:3 - "Therefore with joy shall ye draw water out of the wells of salvation."

Isaiah 29:19 - "The meek also shall increase their joy in the LORD..."

Isaiah 35:10 - "And the ransomed of the LORD shall return, and come to Zion with songs and everlasting joy upon their heads: they shall obtain joy and gladness, and sorrow and sighing shall flee away."

John 15:11 - "These things have I spoken unto you, that my joy might remain in you, and that your joy might be full."

Kindness
Kindness permeates my soul!

Psalm 31:21 - *"Blessed be the LORD: for he hath shewed me his marvellous kindness in a strong city."*

Psalm 36:10 - *"O continue thy lovingkindness unto them that know thee; and thy righteousness to the upright in heart."*

Psalm 40:11 - *"Withhold not thou thy tender mercies from me, O LORD: let thy lovingkindness and thy truth continually preserve me."*

Psalm 103:4 - *"Who redeemeth thy life from destruction; who crowneth thee with lovingkindness and tender mercies;"*

Psalm 117:2 - *"For his merciful kindness is great toward us: and the truth of the LORD endureth for ever. Praise ye the LORD."*

Matthew 25:40 - *"And the King shall answer and say unto them, Verily I say unto you, Inasmuch as ye have done it unto one of the least of these my brethren, ye have done it unto me."*

Kingdom of God
The Kingdom of God lives in me!

Psalm 68:32 - *"Sing unto God, ye kingdoms of the earth; O sing praises unto the Lord; Selah:"*

Matthew 6:33 - *"But seek ye first the kingdom of God, and his righteousness; and all these things shall be added unto you."*

Matthew 12:28 - "But if I cast out devils by the Spirit of God, then the kingdom of God is come unto you."

Luke 8:10 - "And he said, Unto you it is given to know the mysteries of the kingdom of God..."

Luke 9:62 - "And Jesus said unto him, No man, having put his hand to the plough, and looking back, is fit for the kingdom of God."

Luke 12:31 - "But rather seek ye the kingdom of God; and all these things shall be added unto you."

1 Corinthians 4:20 - "For the kingdom of God is not in word, but in power."

Knowledge
Knowledge is power!

Genesis 2:17 - "But of the tree of the knowledge of good and evil, thou shalt not eat of it: for in the day that thou eatest thereof thou shalt surely die."

Exodus 31:3 - "And I have filled him with the spirit of God, in wisdom, and in understanding, and in knowledge, and in all manner of workmanship,"

Psalm 119:66 - "Teach me good judgment and knowledge: for I have believed thy commandments."

Proverbs 1:7 - "The fear of the LORD is the beginning of knowledge: but fools despise wisdom and instruction."

Proverbs 2:6 - "For the LORD giveth wisdom: out of his mouth cometh knowledge and understanding."

Proverbs 9:10 - "The fear of the LORD is the beginning of wisdom: and the knowledge of the holy is understanding."

2 Timothy 2:7 - "Consider what I say; and the Lord give thee understanding in all things."

Laughter
Laughter is good for the soul!

Job 8:21 - "Till he fill thy mouth with laughing, and thy lips with rejoicing."

Psalm 59:8 - "But thou, O LORD, shalt laugh at them; thou shalt have all the heathen in derision."

Psalm 126:2 - "Then was our mouth filled with laughter, and our tongue with singing: then said they among the heathen, The LORD hath done great things for them."

Proverbs 14:13 - "Even in laughter the heart is sorrowful; and the end of that mirth is heaviness."

Ecclesiastes 3:4 - "A time to weep, and a time to laugh; a time to mourn, and a time to dance;"

Ecclesiastes 7:3 - "Sorrow is better than laughter: for by the sadness of the countenance the heart is made better."

Luke 6:21 - "Blessed are ye that hunger now: for ye shall be filled. Blessed are ye that weep now: for ye shall laugh."

Life

Jesus is the way, the truth and the life...

Deuteronomy 30:15 - *"See, I have set before thee this day life and good, and death and evil;"*

Deuteronomy 30:19 - *"I call heaven and earth to record this day against you, that I have set before you life and death, blessing and cursing: therefore choose life, that both thou and thy seed may live:"*

Ruth 4:15 - *"And he shall be unto thee a restorer of thy life, and a nourisher of thine old age:"*

Job 33:4 - *"The spirit of God hath made me, and the breath of the Almighty hath given me life."*

Psalm 103:4 - *"Who redeemeth thy life from destruction; who crowneth thee with lovingkindness and tender mercies;"*

Proverbs 18:21 - *"Death and life are in the power of the tongue: and they that love it shall eat the fruit thereof."*

John 14:6 - *"Jesus saith unto him, I am the way, the truth, and the life: no man cometh unto the Father, but by me."*

Life - Giving

God is the giver of Life!

Matthew 7:17 - *"Even so every good tree bringeth forth good fruit; but a corrupt tree bringeth forth evil fruit."*

Luke 6:45 - "A good man out of the good treasure of his heart bringeth forth that which is good; and an evil man out of the evil treasure of his heart bringeth forth that which is evil: for of the abundance of the heart his mouth speaketh."

John 6:48 - "I am that bread of life."

John 10:10 - "The thief cometh not, but for to steal, and to kill, and to destroy: I am come that they might have life, and that they might have it more abundantly."

John 10:28 - "And I give unto them eternal life; and they shall never perish, neither shall any man pluck them out of my hand."

John 12:25 - "He that loveth his life shall lose it; and he that hateth his life in this world shall keep it unto life eternal."

Listening
I am a good listener!

Job 33:8 - "Surely thou hast spoken in mine hearing, and I have heard the voice of thy words..."

Psalm 143:8 - "Cause me to hear thy lovingkindness in the morning; for in thee do I trust: cause me to know the way wherein I should walk; for I lift up my soul unto thee."

Matthew 13:43 - "Then shall the righteous shine forth as the sun in the kingdom of their Father. Who hath ears to hear, let him hear."

Luke 8:10 - "And he said, Unto you it is given to know the mysteries of the kingdom of God: but to others in parables; that seeing they might not see, and hearing they might not understand."

John 8:47 - "He that is of God heareth God's words: ye therefore hear them not, because ye are not of God. He that is of God heareth God's words: ye therefore hear them not, because ye are not of God."

Romans 10:17 - "So then faith cometh by hearing, and hearing by the word of God."

Love

I am loved by God!

Deuteronomy 11:1 - "Therefore thou shalt love the LORD thy God, and keep his charge, and his statutes, and his judgments, and his commandments, alway."

Joshua 23:11 - "Take good heed therefore unto yourselves, that ye love the LORD your God."

Isaiah 43:4 - "Since thou wast precious in my sight, thou hast been honourable, and I have loved thee: therefore will I give men for thee, and people for thy life."

Psalm 91:14 - "Because he hath set his love upon me, therefore will I deliver him: I will set him on high, because he hath known my name."

Proverbs 8:17 - "I love them that love me; and those that seek me early shall find me."

Proverbs 10:12 - "Hatred stirreth up strifes: but love covereth all sins."

Song of Solomon 2:6 - "His left hand is under my head, and his right hand doth embrace me."

Song of Solomon 7:10 - "I am my beloved's, and his desire is toward me."

Matthew 5:44 - "But I say unto you, Love your enemies, bless them that curse you, do good to them that hate you, and pray for them which despitefully use you, and persecute you;"

John 13:34 - "A new commandment I give unto you, That ye love one another; as I have loved you, that ye also love one another."

Romans 12:10 - "Be kindly affectioned one to another with brotherly love; in honour preferring one another;"

1 Corinthians 13:4-8 - "Now there are diversities of gifts, but the same Spirit. And there are differences of administrations, but the same Lord. And there are diversities of operations, but it is the same God which worketh all in all. But the manifestation of the Spirit is given to every man to profit withal. For to one is given by the Spirit the word of wisdom; to another the word of knowledge by the same Spirit;"

Ephesians 4:29 - "Let no corrupt communication proceed out of your mouth, but that which is good to the use of edifying, that it may minister grace unto the hearers."

Philippians 4:1 - "Therefore, my brethren dearly beloved and longed for, my joy and crown, so stand fast in the Lord, my dearly beloved."

1 Thessalonians 3:12 - "And the Lord make you to increase and abound in love one toward another, and toward all men, even as we do toward you:"

1 John 1:6 - "If we say that we have fellowship with him, and walk in darkness, we lie, and do not the truth:"

1 John 2:5 - "But whoso keepeth his word, in him verily is the love of God perfected: hereby know we that we are in him."

1 John 4:7-8 - "Beloved, let us love one another: for love is of God; and every one that loveth is born of God, and knoweth God. He that loveth not knoweth not God; for God is love."

1 John 4:18 - "There is no fear in love; but perfect love casteth out fear: because fear hath torment. He that feareth is not made perfect in love."

2 John 1:3 - "Grace be with you, mercy, and peace, from God the Father, and from the Lord Jesus Christ, the Son of the Father, in truth and love."

Love of God
God's love makes me complete!

Psalm 70:4 - "Let all those that seek thee rejoice and be glad in thee: and let such as love thy salvation say continually, Let God be magnified."

Hosea 14:4 - "I will heal their backsliding, I will love them freely: for mine anger is turned away from him."

Romans 5:5 - "And hope maketh not ashamed; because the love of God is shed abroad in our hearts by the Holy Ghost which is given unto us."

Romans 5:8 - "But God commendeth his love toward us, in that, while we were yet sinners, Christ died for us."

Romans 8:39 - "Nor height, nor depth, nor any other creature, shall be able to separate us from the love of God, which is in Christ Jesus our Lord."

1 Corinthians 2:9 - "But as it is written, Eye hath not seen, nor ear heard, neither have entered into the heart of man, the things which God hath prepared for them that love him."

2 Timothy 1:7 - "For God hath not given us the spirit of fear; but of power, and of love, and of a sound mind."

Lust
I am free from the spirit of lust!

Galatians 5:16 - "This I say then, Walk in the Spirit, and ye shall not fulfil the lust of the flesh."

Titus 2:12 - "Teaching us that, denying ungodliness and worldly lusts, we should live soberly, righteously, and godly, in this present world;"

James 1:15 - "Then when lust hath conceived, it bringeth forth sin: and sin, when it is finished, bringeth forth death."

1 Peter 2:11 - "Dearly beloved, I beseech you as strangers and pilgrims, abstain from fleshly lusts, which war against the soul;"

2 Peter 1:4 - "Whereby are given unto us exceeding great and precious promises: that by these ye might be partakers of the divine nature, having escaped the corruption that is in the world through lust."

1 John 2:16 - "For all that is in the world, the lust of the flesh, and the lust of the eyes, and the pride of life, is not of the Father, but is of the world."

Marriage
I will live a God-ordained marriage!

Matthew 22:2 - "The kingdom of heaven is like unto a certain king, which made a marriage for his son,"

1 Corinthians 7:34 - "There is difference also between a wife and a virgin. The unmarried woman careth for the things of the Lord, that she may be holy both in body and in spirit: but she that is married careth for the things of the world, how she may please her husband."

1 Corinthians 7:38 - "So then he that giveth her in marriage doeth well; but he that giveth her not in marriage doeth better."

Ephesians 5:31 - "For this cause shall a man leave his father and mother, and shall be joined unto his wife, and they two shall be one flesh."

Hebrews 13:4 - "Marriage is honourable in all, and the bed undefiled: but whoremongers and adulterers God will judge."

Revelation 19:7 - "Let us be glad and rejoice, and give honour to him: for the marriage of the Lamb is come, and his wife hath made herself ready."

Mercy
God's mercy is forever!

Numbers 14:18 - "The LORD is longsuffering, and of great mercy, forgiving iniquity and transgression, and by no means clearing the guilty..."

Deuteronomy 5:10 - "And shewing mercy unto thousands of them that love me and keep my commandments."

1 Chronicles 16:34 - "O give thanks unto the LORD; for he is good; for his mercy endureth for ever."

Psalm 6:2 - "Have mercy upon me, O LORD; for I am weak: O LORD, heal me; for my bones are vexed."

Psalm 33:18 - "Behold, the eye of the LORD is upon them that fear him, upon them that hope in his mercy;"

Psalm 57:10 - "For thy mercy is great unto the heavens, and thy truth unto the clouds."

Psalm 103:4 - "Who redeemeth thy life from destruction; who crowneth thee with lovingkindness and tender mercies;"

Jude 1:21 - "Keep yourselves in the love of God, looking for the mercy of our Lord Jesus Christ unto eternal life."

Mind of Christ
I have the Mind of Christ!

Psalm 71:1 - "In thee, O LORD, do I put my trust: let me never be put to confusion."

Romans 7:25 - "I thank God through Jesus Christ our Lord. So then with the mind I myself serve the law of God;"

Romans 8:6 - "For to be carnally minded is death; but to be spiritually minded is life and peace."

Ephesians 4:22-24 - "That ye put off concerning the former conversation the old man, which is corrupt according to the deceitful lusts; And be renewed in the spirit of your mind; And that ye put on the new man, which after God is created in righteousness and true holiness."

Colossians 3:10 - "And have put on the new man, which is renewed in knowledge after the image of him that created him:"

2 Timothy 1:7 - "For God hath not given us the spirit of fear; but of power, and of love, and of a sound mind."

James 1:8 - "A double minded man is unstable in all his ways."

New Wine
God has filled me with New Wine!

Psalm 4:7 - "Thou hast put gladness in my heart, more than in the time that their corn and their wine increased."

Proverbs 3:10 - "So shall thy barns be filled with plenty, and thy presses shall burst out with new wine."

Song of Solomon 1:4 - "Draw me, we will run after thee: the king hath brought me into his chambers: we will be glad and rejoice in thee, we will remember thy love more than wine: the upright love thee."

Matthew 9:17 - "Neither do men put new wine into old bottles: else the bottles break, and the wine runneth out, and the bottles perish: but they put new wine into new bottles, and both are preserved."

Luke 5:38 - "But new wine must be put into new bottles; and both are preserved."

1 Corinthians 10:4 - "And did all drink the same spiritual drink: for they drank of that spiritual Rock that followed them: and that Rock was Christ."

Obedience

I choose to walk in Obedience!

Deuteronomy 11:27 - *"A blessing, if ye obey the commandments of the LORD your God, which I command you this day:"*

Deuteronomy 30:20 - *"That thou mayest love the LORD thy God, and that thou mayest obey his voice, and that thou mayest cleave unto him: for he is thy life, and the length of thy days: that thou mayest dwell in the land which the LORD sware unto thy fathers, to Abraham, to Isaac, and to Jacob, to give them."*

1 Samuel 12:14 - *"If ye will fear the LORD, and serve him, and obey his voice, and not rebel against the commandment of the LORD, then shall both ye and also the king that reigneth over you continue following the LORD your God:"*

1 Samuel 15:22 - *"And Samuel said, Hath the LORD as great delight in burnt offerings and sacrifices, as in obeying the voice of the LORD? Behold, to obey is better than sacrifice, and to hearken than the fat of rams."*

Psalm 37:5 - *"Commit thy way unto the LORD; trust also in him; and he shall bring it to pass."*

Isaiah 1:19 - *"If ye be willing and obedient, ye shall eat the good of the land:"*

Romans 5:19 - *"For as by one man's disobedience many were made sinners, so by the obedience of one shall many be made righteous."*

2 Corinthians 10:5 - *"Casting down imaginations, and every high thing that exalteth itself against the knowledge of God, and bringing into captivity every thought to the obedience of Christ;"*

Ephesians 5:6 - "Let no man deceive you with vain words: for because of these things cometh the wrath of God upon the children of disobedience."

Hebrews 5:8 - "Though he were a Son, yet learned he obedience by the things which he suffered;"

James 1:22 - "But be ye doers of the word, and not hearers only, deceiving your own selves."

1 John 3:22 - "And whatsoever we ask, we receive of him, because we keep his commandments, and do those things that are pleasing in his sight."

Offense
I choose not to take offense!

Proverbs 18:19 - "A brother offended is harder to be won than a strong city: and their contentions are like the bars of a castle."

Matthew 11:6 - "And blessed is he, whosoever shall not be offended in me."

Matthew 16:23 - "But he turned, and said unto Peter, Get thee behind me, Satan: thou art an offence unto me: for thou savourest not the things that be of God, but those that be of men."

Mark 14:29 - "But Peter said unto him, Although all shall be offended, yet will not I."

Luke 7:23 - "And blessed is he, whosoever shall not be offended in me."

John 16:1 - "These things have I spoken unto you, that ye should not be offended."

Romans 14:21 - *"It is good neither to eat flesh, nor to drink wine, nor any thing whereby thy brother stumbleth, or is offended, or is made weak."*

$\mathcal{O}ffering$
Unto thee O Lord, I give!

Psalm 96:8 - *"Give unto the LORD the glory due unto his name: bring an offering, and come into his courts."*

Mark 12:33 - *"And to love him with all the heart, and with all the understanding, and with all the soul, and with all the strength, and to love his neighbour as himself, is more than all whole burnt offerings and sacrifices."*

Luke 6:38 - *"Give, and it shall be given unto you; good measure, pressed down, and shaken together, and running over, shall men give into your bosom. For with the same measure that ye mete withal it shall be measured to you again."*

Ephesians 5:2 - *"And walk in love, as Christ also hath loved us, and hath given himself for us an offering and a sacrifice to God for a sweetsmelling savour."*

Hebrews 10:10 - *"By the which will we are sanctified through the offering of the body of Jesus Christ once for all."*

Hebrews 10:14 - *"For by one offering he hath perfected for ever them that are sanctified."*

Patience
Patience worketh itself in me!

Psalm 27:14 - *"Wait on the LORD: be of good courage, and he shall strengthen thine heart: wait, I say, on the LORD."*

Lamentations 3:25 - *"The LORD is good unto them that wait for him, to the soul that seeketh him."*

Romans 5:3 - *"And not only so, but we glory in tribulations also: knowing that tribulation worketh patience;"*

Romans 8:25 - *"But if we hope for that we see not, then do we with patience wait for it."*

Romans 15:4 - *"For whatsoever things were written aforetime were written for our learning, that we through patience and comfort of the scriptures might have hope."*

Romans 15:5 - *"Now the God of patience and consolation grant you to be likeminded one toward another according to Christ Jesus:"*

James 1:4 - *"But let patience have her perfect work, that ye may be perfect and entire, wanting nothing."*

Peace
My mind is stayed in perfect peace!

Exodus 14:14 - *"The LORD shall fight for you, and ye shall hold your peace."*

Numbers 6:26 - *"The LORD lift up his countenance upon thee, and give thee peace."*

Isaiah 26:3 - "Thou wilt keep him in perfect peace, whose mind is stayed on thee: because he trusteth in thee."

Isaiah 38:17 - "Behold, for peace I had great bitterness: but thou hast in love to my soul delivered it from the pit of corruption: for thou hast cast all my sins behind thy back."

Jeremiah 29:11-13 - "For I know the thoughts that I think toward you, saith the LORD, thoughts of peace, and not of evil, to give you an expected end. Then shall ye call upon me, and ye shall go and pray unto me, and I will hearken unto you. And ye shall seek me, and find me, when ye shall search for me with all your heart."

Job 13:5 - "O that ye would altogether hold your peace! and it should be your wisdom."

Psalm 4:8 - "I will both lay me down in peace, and sleep: for thou, LORD, only makest me dwell in safety."

Psalm 29:11 - "The LORD will give strength unto his people; the LORD will bless his people with peace."

Psalm 34:14 - "Depart from evil, and do good; seek peace, and pursue it."

Psalm 37:11 - "But the meek shall inherit the earth; and shall delight themselves in the abundance of peace."

Psalm 55:18 - "He hath delivered my soul in peace from the battle that was against me: for there were many with me."

John 14:27 - "Peace I leave with you, my peace I give unto you: not as the world giveth, give I unto you. Let not your heart be troubled, neither let it be afraid."

Philippians 4:7 - "And the peace of God, which passeth all understanding, shall keep your hearts and minds through Christ Jesus."

Colossians 3:15 - "And let the peace of God rule in your hearts, to the which also ye are called in one body; and be ye thankful."

$\mathcal{P}oison$
My tongue shall speak blessings!

Job 27:4 - "My lips shall not speak wickedness, nor my tongue utter deceit."

Psalm 34:13 - "Keep thy tongue from evil, and thy lips from speaking guile."

Psalm 58:4 - "Their poison is like the poison of a serpent: they are like the deaf adder that stoppeth her ear;"

Psalm 140:3 - "They have sharpened their tongues like a serpent; adders' poison is under their lips. Selah."

Romans 3:13 - "Their throat is an open sepulchre; with their tongues they have used deceit; the poison of asps is under their lips:"

James 3:6-8 - "And the tongue is a fire, a world of iniquity: so is the tongue among our members, that it defileth the whole body, and setteth on fire the course of nature; and it is set on fire of hell. For every kind of beasts, and of birds, and of serpents, and of things in the sea, is tamed, and hath been tamed of mankind: But the tongue can no man tame; it is an unruly evil, full of deadly poison."

Power of God
The power of God worketh itself in me!

Psalm 68:35 - "O God, thou art terrible out of thy holy places: the God of Israel is he that giveth strength and power unto his people. Blessed be God."

Daniel 2:37 - "Thou, O king, art a king of kings: for the God of heaven hath given thee a kingdom, power, and strength, and glory."

Luke 22:69 - "Hereafter shall the Son of man sit on the right hand of the power of God."

Acts 10:38 - "How God anointed Jesus of Nazareth with the Holy Ghost and with power: who went about doing good, and healing all that were oppressed of the devil; for God was with him."

1 Corinthians 6:14 - "And God hath both raised up the Lord, and will also raise up us by his own power."

2 Corinthians 4:7 - "But we have this treasure in earthen vessels, that the excellency of the power may be of God, and not of us."

Praise
Praise shall continually be in my mouth!

2 Samuel 22:4 - "I will call on the LORD, who is worthy to be praised: so shall I be saved from mine enemies."

1 Chronicles 16:25 - "For great is the LORD, and greatly to be praised: he also is to be feared above all gods."

1 Chronicles 23:30 - "And to stand every morning to thank and praise the LORD,"

1 Chronicles 29:13 - "Now therefore, our God, we thank thee, and praise thy glorious name."

Psalm 7:17 - "I will praise the LORD according to his righteousness: and will sing praise to the name of the LORD most high."

Psalm 9:1 - "I will praise thee, O LORD, with my whole heart; I will shew forth all thy marvellous works."

Psalm 28:7 - "The LORD is my strength and my shield; my heart trusted in him, and I am helped: therefore my heart greatly rejoiceth; and with my song will I praise him."

Psalm 34:1 - "I will bless the LORD at all times: his praise shall continually be in my mouth."

Psalm 42:5 - "Why art thou cast down, O my soul? and why art thou disquieted in me? hope thou in God: for I shall yet praise him for the help of his countenance."

Isaiah 42:10 - "Sing unto the LORD a new song, and his praise from the end of the earth, ye that go down to the sea, and all that is therein; the isles, and the inhabitants thereof."

Psalm 100:1 - "Make a joyful noise unto the LORD, all ye lands."

Psalm 104:33 - "I will sing unto the LORD as long as I live: I will sing praise to my God while I have my being."

Psalm 145:2 - "Every day will I bless thee; and I will praise thy name for ever and ever."

Psalm 146:2 - "While I live will I praise the LORD: I will sing praises unto my God while I have any being."

1 Peter 3:12 - "For the eyes of the Lord are over the righteous, and his ears are open unto their prayers: but the face of the Lord is against them that do evil."

Prayer
Prayer changes me!

Psalm 4:1 - "Hear me when I call, O God of my righteousness: thou hast enlarged me when I was in distress; have mercy upon me, and hear my prayer."

Psalm 5:3 - "My voice shalt thou hear in the morning, O LORD; in the morning will I direct my prayer unto thee, and will look up."

Psalm 6:9 - "The LORD hath heard my supplication; the LORD will receive my prayer."

Psalm 22:24 - "For he hath not despised nor abhorred the affliction of the afflicted; neither hath he hid his face from him; but when he cried unto him, he heard."

Psalm 42:8 - "Yet the LORD will command his lovingkindness in the day time, and in the night his song shall be with me, and my prayer unto the God of my life."

Psalm 138:3 - "In the day when I cried thou answeredst me, and strengthenedst me with strength in my soul."

Proverbs 15:8 - "The sacrifice of the wicked is an abomination to the LORD: but the prayer of the upright is his delight."

Matthew 6:8 - "Be not ye therefore like unto them: for your Father knoweth what things ye have need of, before ye ask him."

Matthew 7:7-8 - "Ask, and it shall be given you; seek, and ye shall find; knock, and it shall be opened unto you: For every one that asketh receiveth; and he that seeketh findeth; and to him that knocketh it shall be opened."

Matthew 21:22 - "And all things, whatsoever ye shall ask in prayer, believing, ye shall receive."

Luke 11:9 - "And I say unto you, Ask, and it shall be given you; seek, and ye shall find; knock, and it shall be opened unto you."

John 14:13 - "And whatsoever ye shall ask in my name, that will I do, that the Father may be glorified in the Son."

Philippians 4:6 - "Be careful for nothing; but in everything by prayer and supplication with thanksgiving let your requests be made known unto God."

1 Thessalonians 5:17 - "Pray without ceasing."

James 5:13 - "Is any among you afflicted? let him pray. Is any merry? let him sing psalms."

Preserved
I am preserved for God's purpose!

Deuteronomy 6:24 - "And the LORD commanded us to do all these statutes, to fear the LORD our God, for our good always, that he might preserve us alive, as it is at this day."

Job 10:12 - "Thou hast granted me life and favour, and thy visitation hath preserved my spirit."

Psalm 12:7 - "Thou shalt keep them, O LORD, thou shalt preserve them from this generation for ever."

Psalm 16:1 - "Preserve me, O God: for in thee do I put my trust."

Psalm 25:21 - "Let integrity and uprightness preserve me; for I wait on thee."

Psalm 32:7 - "Thou art my hiding place; thou shalt preserve me from trouble; thou shalt compass me about with songs of deliverance. Selah."

Luke 5:38 - "But new wine must be put into new bottles; and both are preserved."

Promise

I am standing on the Promises of God!

Isaiah 65:17 - "For, behold, I create new heavens and a new earth: and the former shall not be remembered, nor come into mind."

Joel 2:25-26 - "And I will restore to you the years that the locust hath eaten, the cankerworm, and the caterpiller, and the palmerworm, my great army which I sent among you. And ye shall eat in plenty, and be satisfied, and praise the name of the LORD your God, that hath dealt wondrously with you: and my people shall never be ashamed."

Malachi 3:10 - "Bring ye all the tithes into the storehouse, that there may be meat in mine house, and prove me now herewith, saith the LORD of hosts, if I will not open you the windows of heaven, and pour you out a blessing, that there shall not be room enough to receive it."

John 14:16 - "And I will pray the Father, and he shall give you another Comforter, that he may abide with you for ever;"

John 14:21 - "He that hath my commandments, and keepeth them, he it is that loveth me: and he that loveth me shall be loved of my Father, and I will love him, and will manifest myself to him."

Luke 24:49 - "And, behold, I send the promise of my Father upon you: but tarry ye in the city of Jerusalem, until ye be endued with power from on high."

Acts 2:39 - "For the promise is unto you, and to your children, and to all that are afar off, even as many as the LORD our God shall call."

Acts 26:16 - "But rise, and stand upon thy feet: for I have appeared unto thee for this purpose, to make thee a minister and a witness both of these things which thou hast seen, and of those things in the which I will appear unto thee;"

Romans 4:21 - "And being fully persuaded that, what he had promised, he was able also to perform."

2 Corinthians 1:20 - "For all the promises of God in him are yea, and in him Amen, unto the glory of God by us."

2 Corinthians 7:1 - "Having therefore these promises, dearly beloved, let us cleanse ourselves from all filthiness of the flesh and spirit, perfecting holiness in the fear of God."

Ephesians 1:13 - "In whom ye also trusted, after that ye heard the word of truth, the gospel of your salvation: in whom also after that ye believed, ye were sealed with that holy Spirit of promise,"

Ephesians 1:18-19 - "The eyes of your understanding being enlightened; that ye may know what is the hope of his calling, and what the riches of the glory of his inheritance in the saints, And what is the exceeding greatness of his power to us-ward who believe, according to the working of his mighty power,"

1 Timothy 4:8 - "For bodily exercise profiteth little: but godliness is profitable unto all things, having promise of the life that now is, and of that which is to come."

Hebrews 6:12 - "That ye be not slothful, but followers of them who through faith and patience inherit the promises."

James 1:12 - "Blessed is the man that endureth temptation: for when he is tried, he shall receive the crown of life, which the Lord hath promised to them that love him."

James 2:5 - "Hearken, my beloved brethren, Hath not God chosen the poor of this world rich in faith, and heirs of the kingdom which he hath promised to them that love him?"

1 Peter 1:4 - "To an inheritance incorruptible, and undefiled, and that fadeth not away, reserved in heaven for you,"

1 John 5:11 - "And this is the record, that God hath given to us eternal life, and this life is in his Son."

Prosperity

My life prospers by the Word of God!

Job 36:11 - "If they obey and serve him, they shall spend their days in prosperity, and their years in pleasures."

Psalm 35:27 - "Let them shout for joy, and be glad, that favour my righteous cause: yea, let them say continually, Let the LORD be magnified, which hath pleasure in the prosperity of his servant."

Psalm 118:25 - "Save now, I beseech thee, O LORD: O LORD, I beseech thee, send now prosperity."

Psalm 122:7 - "Peace be within thy walls, and prosperity within thy palaces."

Proverbs 28:13 - "He that covereth his sins shall not prosper: but whoso confesseth and forsaketh them shall have mercy."

Isaiah 48:15 - "I, even I, have spoken; yea, I have called him: I have brought him, and he shall make his way prosperous."

Isaiah 55:11 - "So shall my word be that goeth forth out of my mouth: it shall not return unto me void, but it shall accomplish that which I please, and it shall prosper in the thing whereto I sent it."

Protection
God is a shield for me!

2 Samuel 22:3 - "The God of my rock; in him will I trust: he is my shield, and the horn of my salvation, my high tower, and my refuge, my saviour; thou savest me from violence."

Psalm 3:3 - "But thou, O LORD, art a shield for me; my glory, and the lifter up of mine head."

Psalm 5:12 - "For thou, LORD, wilt bless the righteous; with favour wilt thou compass him as with a shield."

Psalm 9:9 - "The LORD also will be a refuge for the oppressed, a refuge in times of trouble."

Psalm 28:7 - "The LORD is my strength and my shield; my heart trusted in him, and I am helped: therefore my heart greatly rejoiceth..."

Psalm 33:20 - "Our soul waiteth for the LORD: he is our help and our shield."

Psalm 84:9 - "Behold, O God our shield, and look upon the face of thine anointed."

Psalm 84:11 - "For the LORD God is a sun and shield: the LORD will give grace and glory: no good thing will he withhold from them that walk uprightly."

Psalm 91:4 - "He shall cover thee with his feathers, and under his wings shalt thou trust: his truth shall be thy shield and buckler."

Isaiah 43:2 - "When thou passest through the waters, I will be with thee; and through the rivers, they shall not overflow thee: when thou walkest through the fire, thou shalt not be burned; neither shall the flame kindle upon thee."

Isaiah 54:17 - "No weapon that is formed against thee shall prosper; and every tongue that shall rise against thee in judgment thou shalt condemn. This is the heritage of the servants of the LORD, and their righteousness is of me, saith the LORD."

Luke 4:10 - "For it is written, He shall give his angels charge over thee, to keep thee:"

2 Corinthians 4:8 - "We are troubled on every side, yet not distressed; we are perplexed, but not in despair;"

2 Thessalonians 3:3 - "But the Lord is faithful, who shall stablish you, and keep you from evil."

Provision
God is My Provider!

1 Chronicles 29:19 - "And give unto Solomon my son a perfect heart, to keep thy commandments, thy testimonies, and thy statutes, and to do all these things, and to build the palace, for the which I have made provision."

Psalm 90:1 - "Lord, thou hast been our dwelling place in all generations."

Psalm 91:1 - "He that dwelleth in the secret place of the most High shall abide under the shadow of the Almighty."

Psalm 132:15 - "I will abundantly bless her provision: I will satisfy her poor with bread."

Isaiah 58:11 - "And the LORD shall guide thee continually, and satisfy thy soul in drought, and make fat thy bones: and thou shalt be like a watered garden, and like a spring of water, whose waters fail not."

Daniel 1:5 - "And the king appointed them a daily provision of the king's meat, and of the wine which he drank: so nourishing them three years, that at the end thereof they might stand before the king."

Matthew 6:25 - "Therefore I say unto you, Take no thought for your life, what ye shall eat, or what ye shall drink; nor yet for your body, what ye shall put on. Is not the life more than meat, and the body than raiment?"

Luke 12:33 - "Sell that ye have, and give alms; provide yourselves bags which wax not old, a treasure in the heavens that faileth not, where no thief approacheth, neither moth corrupteth."

Romans 13:14 - "But put ye on the Lord Jesus Christ, and make not provision for the flesh, to fulfil the lusts thereof."

2 Corinthians 3:5 - "Not that we are sufficient of ourselves to think any thing as of ourselves; but our sufficiency is of God;"

Philippians 4:19 - "But my God shall supply all your need according to his riches in glory by Christ Jesus."

1 Timothy 5:8 - "But if any provide not for his own, and specially for those of his own house, he hath denied the faith, and is worse than an infidel."

Jude 1:24 - "Now unto him that is able to keep you from falling, and to present you faultless before the presence of his glory with exceeding joy,"

Purify
The Blood of Jesus purifies me!

Numbers 19:12 - "He shall purify himself with it on the third day, and on the seventh day he shall be clean: but if he purify not himself the third day, then the seventh day he shall not be clean."

Acts 15:9 - "And put no difference between us and them, purifying their hearts by faith."

Titus 2:14 - "Who gave himself for us, that he might redeem us from all iniquity, and purify unto himself a peculiar people, zealous of good works."

James 4:8 - "Draw nigh to God, and he will draw nigh to you. Cleanse your hands, ye sinners; and purify your hearts, ye double minded."

1 John 1:7 - "But if we walk in the light, as he is in the light, we have fellowship one with another, and the blood of Jesus Christ his Son cleanseth us from all sin."

1 John 1:9 - "If we confess our sins, he is faithful and just to forgive us our sins, and to cleanse us from all unrighteousness."

Purity
In Him all things are pure!

1 Corinthians 6:11 - "And such were some of you: but ye are washed, but ye are sanctified, but ye are justified in the name of the Lord Jesus, and by the Spirit of our God."

1 Peter 1:22 - "Seeing ye have purified your souls in obeying the truth through the Spirit unto unfeigned love of the brethren, see that ye love one another with a pure heart fervently:"

Psalm 12:6 - "The words of the LORD are pure words: as silver tried in a furnace of earth, purified seven times."

Psalm 17:3 - "Thou hast proved mine heart; thou hast visited me in the night; thou hast tried me, and shalt find nothing; I am purposed that my mouth shall not transgress."

Psalm 18:26 - "With the pure thou wilt shew thyself pure; and with the froward thou wilt shew thyself froward."

2 Timothy 1:9 - "Who hath saved us, and called us with an holy calling, not according to our works, but according to his own purpose and grace, which was given us in Christ Jesus before the world began,"

Purpose
I am fulfilling my purpose in God!

Ecclesiastes 3:1 - "Who hath saved us, and called us with an holy calling, not according to our works, but according to his own purpose and grace, which was given us in Christ Jesus before the world began,"

Isaiah 43:18-19 - "Remember ye not the former things, neither consider the things of old. Behold, I will do a new thing; now it shall spring forth; shall ye not know it? I will even make a way in the wilderness, and rivers in the desert."

Proverbs 15:22 - "Without counsel purposes are disappointed: but in the multitude of counsellors they are established."

Romans 8:28 - "And we know that all things work together for good to them that love God, to them who are the called according to his purpose."

2 Corinthians 9:7 - "Every man according as he purposeth in his heart, so let him give; not grudgingly, or of necessity: for God loveth a cheerful giver."

Rebellion

I have been delivered from Rebellion!

1 Samuel 15:23 - "For rebellion is as the sin of witchcraft, and stubbornness is as iniquity and idolatry. Because thou hast rejected the word of the LORD, he hath also rejected thee from being king."

Psalm 68:6 - "God setteth the solitary in families: he bringeth out those which are bound with chains: but the rebellious dwell in a dry land."

Proverbs 17:11 - "An evil man seeketh only rebellion: therefore a cruel messenger shall be sent against him."

Isaiah 50:5 - "The Lord GOD hath opened mine ear, and I was not rebellious, neither turned away back."

Isaiah 65:2 - "I have spread out my hands all the day unto a rebellious people, which walketh in a way that was not good, after their own thoughts;"

Jeremiah 28:16 - "Therefore thus saith the LORD; Behold, I will cast thee from off the face of the earth: this year thou shalt die, because thou hast taught rebellion against the LORD."

Redemption
I am redeemed by God!

Psalm 111:9 - "He sent redemption unto his people: he hath commanded his covenant for ever: holy and reverend is his name."

Matthew 10:39 - "He that findeth his life shall lose it: and he that loseth his life for my sake shall find it."

Luke 21:28 - "And when these things begin to come to pass, then look up, and lift up your heads; for your redemption draweth nigh."

Romans 3:24 - "Being justified freely by his grace through the redemption that is in Christ Jesus:"

1 Corinthians 1:30 - "But of him are ye in Christ Jesus, who of God is made unto us wisdom, and righteousness, and sanctification, and redemption:"

Ephesians 1:7 - "In whom we have redemption through his blood, the forgiveness of sins, according to the riches of his grace;"

Ephesians 4:30 - "And grieve not the holy Spirit of God, whereby ye are sealed unto the day of redemption."

Renewal

My mind is renewed in Christ!

Psalm 103:5 - *"Who satisfieth thy mouth with good things; so that thy youth is renewed like the eagle's."*

Romans 12:2 - *"And be not conformed to this world: but be ye transformed by the renewing of your mind, that ye may prove what is that good, and acceptable, and perfect, will of God."*

2 Corinthians 4:16 - *"For which cause we faint not; but though our outward man perish, yet the inward man is renewed day by day."*

Ephesians 4:23 - *"And be renewed in the spirit of your mind;"*

Colossians 3:10 - *"And have put on the new man, which is renewed in knowledge after the image of him that created him:"*

Titus 3:5 - *"Not by works of righteousness which we have done, but according to his mercy he saved us, by the washing of regeneration, and renewing of the Holy Ghost;"*

Responsibility

I am a responsible child of God!

Leviticus 18:10 - *"The nakedness of thy son's daughter, or of thy daughter's daughter, even their nakedness thou shalt not uncover: for theirs is thine own nakedness."*

Deuteronomy 12:8 - "Ye shall not do after all the things that we do here this day, every man whatsoever is right in his own eyes."

Proverbs 5:15 - "Drink waters out of thine own cistern, and running waters out of thine own well."

Proverbs 8:36 - "But he that sinneth against me wrongeth his own soul: all they that hate me love death."

Luke 6:42 - "... Brother, let me pull out the mote that is in thine eye, when thou thyself beholdest not the beam that is in thine own eye? Thou hypocrite, cast out first the beam out of thine own eye..."

1 Corinthians 6:19 - "What? know ye not that your body is the temple of the Holy Ghost which is in you, which ye have of God, and ye are not your own?"

Rest

I will rest in God's presence!

Genesis 2:3 - "And God blessed the seventh day, and sanctified it: because that in it he had rested from all his work which God created and made."

Exodus 33:14 - "And he said, My presence shall go with thee, and I will give thee rest."

1 Kings 8:56 - "Blessed be the LORD, that hath given rest unto his people Israel, according to all that he promised: there hath not failed one word of all his good promise, which he promised by the hand of Moses his servant."

Psalm 23:5 - "Thou preparest a table before me in the presence of mine enemies:"

Zephaniah 3:17 - "The LORD thy God in the midst of thee is mighty; he will save, he will rejoice over thee with joy; he will rest in his love, he will joy over thee with singing."

Matthew 11:28-30 - "Come unto me, all ye that labour and are heavy laden, and I will give you rest. Take my yoke upon you, and learn of me; for I am meek and lowly in heart: and ye shall find rest unto your souls. For my yoke is easy, and my burden is light."

Righteousness
I am the Righteousness of God!

Psalm 11:7 - "For the righteous LORD loveth righteousness; his countenance doth behold the upright."

Psalm 17:15 - "As for me, I will behold thy face in righteousness: I shall be satisfied, when I awake, with thy likeness."

Psalm 37:17 - "For the arms of the wicked shall be broken: but the LORD upholdeth the righteous."

Psalm 37:23 - "The steps of a good man are ordered by the LORD: and he delighteth in his way."

Psalm 112:1-3 - "Praise ye the LORD. Blessed is the man that feareth the LORD, that delighteth greatly in his commandments. His seed shall be mighty upon earth: the generation of the upright shall be blessed. Wealth and riches shall be in his house: and his righteousness endureth for ever."

Psalm 140:13 - "Surely the righteous shall give thanks unto thy name: the upright shall dwell in thy presence."

Proverbs 15:6 - "In the house of the righteous is much treasure: but in the revenues of the wicked is trouble."

Matthew 6:33 - "But seek ye first the kingdom of God, and his righteousness; and all these things shall be added unto you."

Romans 6:18 - "Being then made free from sin, ye became the servants of righteousness."

Romans 14:17 - "For the kingdom of God is not meat and drink; but righteousness, and peace, and joy in the Holy Ghost."

2 Corinthians 5:21 - "For he hath made him to be sin for us, who knew no sin; that we might be made the righteousness of God in him."

Galatians 5:17 - "For the flesh lusteth against the Spirit, and the Spirit against the flesh: and these are contrary the one to the other: so that ye cannot do the things that ye would."

Philippians 1:11 - "Being filled with the fruits of righteousness, which are by Jesus Christ, unto the glory and praise of God."

James 5:16 - "... The effectual fervent prayer of a righteous man availeth much."

Salvation

Praise God for my soul salvation!

Deuteronomy 20:4 - "For the LORD your God is he that goeth with you, to fight for you against your enemies, to save you."

Psalm 13:5 - "But I have trusted in thy mercy; my heart shall rejoice in thy salvation."

Psalm 18:2 - "The LORD is my rock, and my fortress, and my deliverer; my God, my strength, in whom I will trust; my buckler, and the horn of my salvation, and my high tower."

Psalm 21:5 - "His glory is great in thy salvation: honour and majesty hast thou laid upon him."

Psalm 34:18 - "The LORD is nigh unto them that are of a broken heart; and saveth such as be of a contrite spirit."

Psalm 35:9 - "And my soul shall be joyful in the LORD: it shall rejoice in his salvation."

Psalm 51:12 - "Restore unto me the joy of thy salvation; and uphold me with thy free spirit."

Psalm 62:1 - "Truly my soul waiteth upon God: from him cometh my salvation."

Psalm 86:7 - "In the day of my trouble I will call upon thee: for thou wilt answer me."

Psalm 89:26 - "He shall cry unto me, Thou art my father, my God, and the rock of my salvation."

Psalm 121:7 - "The LORD shall preserve thee from all evil: he shall preserve thy soul."

Psalm 138:7 - "Though I walk in the midst of trouble, thou wilt revive me: thou shalt stretch forth thine hand against the wrath of mine enemies, and thy right hand shall save me."

Psalm 139:14 - "I will praise thee; for I am fearfully and wonderfully made: marvellous are thy works; and that my soul knoweth right well."

Proverbs 21:23 - "Whoso keepeth his mouth and his tongue keepeth his soul from troubles."

Isaiah 12:2 - "Behold, God is my salvation; I will trust, and not be afraid: for the LORD JEHOVAH is my strength and my song; he also is become my salvation."

Isaiah 61:10 - "I will greatly rejoice in the LORD, my soul shall be joyful in my God; for he hath clothed me with the garments of salvation, he hath covered me with the robe of righteousness,"

Matthew 16:26 - "For what is a man profited, if he shall gain the whole world, and lose his own soul? or what shall a man give in exchange for his soul?"

John 8:12 - "Then spake Jesus again unto them, saying, I am the light of the world: he that followeth me shall not walk in darkness, but shall have the light of life."

John 14:6 - "Jesus saith unto him, I am the way, the truth, and the life: no man cometh unto the Father, but by me."

Galatians 2:20 - "I am crucified with Christ: neverthless I live; yet not I, but Christ liveth in me: and the life which I now live in the flesh I live by the faith of the Son of God, who loved me, and gave himself for me."

Hebrews 7:25 - "Wherefore he is able also to save them to the uttermost that come unto God by him, seeing he ever liveth to make intercession for them."

1 Peter 2:25 - "For ye were as sheep going astray; but are now returned unto the Shepherd and Bishop of your souls."

Saviour
Jesus...the Saviour of my soul!

Isaiah 43:11 - "I, even I, am the LORD; and beside me there is no saviour."

Hosea 13:4 - "Yet I am the LORD thy God from the land of Egypt, and thou shalt know no god but me: for there is no saviour beside me."

Luke 1:47 - "And my spirit hath rejoiced in God my Saviour."

Acts 5:31 - "Him hath God exalted with his right hand to be a Prince and a Saviour, for to give repentance to Israel, and forgiveness of sins."

Ephesians 5:23 - "For the husband is the head of the wife, even as Christ is the head of the church: and he is the saviour of the body."

Titus 2:13 - "Looking for that blessed hope, and the glorious appearing of the great God and our Saviour Jesus Christ;"

1 John 4:4 - "Ye are of God, little children, and have overcome them: because greater is he that is in you, than he that is in the world."

Second Coming
Jesus is here!

John 3:3 - "Jesus answered and said unto him, Verily, verily, I say unto thee, Except a man be born again, he cannot see the kingdom of God."

Philippians 1:26 - "Yet I am the LORD thy God from the land of Egypt, and thou shalt know no god but me: for there is no saviour beside me."

1 Thessalonians 3:13 - "To the end he may stablish your hearts unblameable in holiness before God, even our Father, at the coming of our Lord Jesus Christ with all his saints."

1 Thessalonians 5:23 - "And the very God of peace sanctify you wholly; and I pray God your whole spirit and soul and body be preserved blameless unto the coming of our Lord Jesus Christ."

1 Timothy 4:13 - "Till I come, give attendance to reading, to exhortation, to doctrine."

Hebrews 9:28 - "So Christ was once offered to bear the sins of many; and unto them that look for him shall he appear the second time without sin unto salvation."

Secrets
Jesus is my secret!

Daniel 2:47 - "The king answered unto Daniel, and said, Of a truth it is, that your God is a God of gods, and a Lord of kings, and a revealer of secrets, seeing thou couldest reveal this secret."

Psalm 25:14 - "The secret of the LORD is with them that fear him; and he will shew them his covenant."

Psalm 44:21 - "Shall not God search this out? for he knoweth the secrets of the heart."

Psalm 91:1 - "He that dwelleth in the secret place of the most High shall abide under the shadow of the Almighty."

Proverbs 11:13 - "A talebearer revealeth secrets: but he that is of a faithful spirit concealeth the matter."

Luke 8:17 - "For nothing is secret, that shall not be made manifest; neither any thing hid, that shall not be known and come abroad."

Romans 2:16 - "In the day when God shall judge the secrets of men by Jesus Christ according to my gospel."

Seeking
I will seek Him until I am found!

1 Chronicles 16:11 - "Seek the LORD and his strength, seek his face continually."

Hosea 10:12 - "Sow to yourselves in righteousness, reap in mercy; break up your fallow ground: for it is time to seek the LORD, till he come and rain righteousness upon you."

Psalm 22:1 - "My God, my God, why hast thou forsaken me? why art thou so far from helping me, and from the words of my roaring?"

Psalm 27:4 - "One thing have I desired of the LORD, that will I seek after; that I may dwell in the house of the LORD all the days of my life, to behold the beauty of the LORD, and to enquire in his temple."

Matthew 12:43 - "When the unclean spirit is gone out of a man, he walketh through dry places, seeking rest, and findeth none."

1 Peter 5:8 - "Be sober, be vigilant; because your adversary the devil, as a roaring lion, walketh about, seeking whom he may devour:"

Sexuality
My sexuality is made pure!

Proverbs 5:15 - *"Drink waters out of thine own cistern, and running waters out of thine own well."*

1 Timothy 5:22 - *"Lay hands suddenly on no man, neither be partaker of other men's sins: keep thyself pure."*

2 Timothy 2:22 - *"Flee also youthful lusts: but follow righteousness, faith, charity, peace, with them that call on the Lord out of a pure heart."*

Titus 1:15 - *"Unto the pure all things are pure: but unto them that are defiled and unbelieving is nothing pure; but even their mind and conscience is defiled."*

Hebrews 10:22 - *"Let us draw near with a true heart in full assurance of faith, having our hearts sprinkled from an evil conscience, and our bodies washed with pure water."*

James 1:27 - *"Pure religion and undefiled before God and the Father is this, To visit the fatherless and widows in their affliction, and to keep himself unspotted from the world."*

Shame
Shame is defeated by God's love for me!

Psalm 6:10 - *"Let all mine enemies be ashamed and sore vexed: let them return and be ashamed suddenly."*

Psalm 25:2 - *"O my God, I trust in thee: let me not be ashamed, let not mine enemies triumph over me."*

Psalm 25:20 - "O keep my soul, and deliver me: let me not be ashamed; for I put my trust in thee."

Psalm 31:1 - "In thee, O LORD, do I put my trust; let me never be ashamed: deliver me in thy righteousness."

Psalm 71:24 - "My tongue also shall talk of thy righteousness all the day long: for they are confounded, for they are brought unto shame, that seek my hurt."

Proverbs 13:18 - "Poverty and shame shall be to him that refuseth instruction: but he that regardeth reproof shall be honoured."

Isaiah 41:11 - "Behold, all they that were incensed against thee shall be ashamed and confounded: they shall be as nothing; and they that strive with thee shall perish."

Isaiah 50:7 - "For the Lord GOD will help me; therefore shall I not be confounded: therefore have I set my face like a flint, and I know that I shall not be ashamed."

Isaiah 54:4 - "Fear not; for thou shalt not be ashamed: neither be thou confounded; for thou shalt not be put to shame: for thou shalt forget the shame of thy youth..."

Isaiah 61:7 - "For your shame ye shall have double; and for confusion they shall rejoice in their portion: therefore in their land they shall possess the double: everlasting joy shall be unto them."

Obadiah 1:10 - "For thy violence against thy brother Jacob shame shall cover thee, and thou shalt be cut off for ever."

Mark 8:38 - "Whosoever therefore shall be ashamed of me and of my words in this adulterous and sinful generation; of him also shall the Son of man be ashamed, when he cometh in the glory of his Father with the holy angels."

2 Timothy 2:15 - "Study to shew thyself approved unto God, a workman that needeth not to be ashamed, rightly dividing the word of truth."

Sin

My focus is on the Christ nature of my being!

Exodus 20:5 - "Thou shalt not bow down thyself to them, nor serve them: for I the LORD thy God am a jealous God, visiting the iniquity of the fathers upon the children unto the third and fourth generation of them that hate me;"

Proverbs 17:9 - "He that covereth a transgression seeketh love; but he that repeateth a matter separateth very friends."

Isaiah 1:18 - "Come now, and let us reason together, saith the LORD: though your sins be as scarlet, they shall be as white as snow; though they be red like crimson, they shall be as wool."

Mark 7:15 - "There is nothing from without a man, that entering into him can defile him: but the things which come out of him, those are they that defile the man."

John 3:19 - "And this is the condemnation, that light is come into the world, and men loved darkness rather than light, because their deeds were evil."

Romans 5:8 - "But God commendeth his love toward us, in that, while we were yet sinners, Christ died for us."

$\mathscr{S}inging$
Singing brings healing to my soul!

Isaiah 49:13 - "Sing, O heavens; and be joyful, O earth; and break forth into singing, O mountains: for the LORD hath comforted his people, and will have mercy upon his afflicted."

Psalm 100:2 - "Serve the LORD with gladness: come before his presence with singing."

Psalm 126:2 - "Then was our mouth filled with laughter, and our tongue with singing: then said they among the heathen, The LORD hath done great things for them."

Zephaniah 3:17 - "The LORD thy God in the midst of thee is mighty; he will save, he will rejoice over thee with joy; he will rest in his love, he will joy over thee with singing."

Ephesians 5:19 - "Speaking to yourselves in psalms and hymns and spiritual songs, singing and making melody in your heart to the Lord;"

James 5:13 - "Is any among you afflicted? let him pray. Is any merry? let him sing psalms."

Son of God
I am a Son of God through Christ Jesus!

Matthew 27:43 - "He trusted in God; let him deliver him now, if he will have him: for he said, I am the Son of God."

Luke 1:35 - "...The Holy Ghost shall come upon thee, and the power of the Highest shall overshadow thee: therefore also that holy thing which shall be born of thee shall be called the Son of God."

Luke 9:58 - "And Jesus said unto him, Foxes have holes, and birds of the air have nests; but the Son of man hath not where to lay his head."

John 3:16 - "For God so loved the world, that he gave his only begotten Son, that whosoever believeth in him should not perish, but have everlasting life."

Romans 8:14 - "For as many as are led by the Spirit of God, they are the sons of God."

1 John 3:1 - "Behold, what manner of love the Father hath bestowed upon us, that we should be called the sons of God: therefore the world knoweth us not, because it knew him not."

Sonship
God made me an Overcomer!

Proverbs 23:26 - "My son, give me thine heart, and let thine eyes observe my ways."

Matthew 3:17 - "And lo a voice from heaven, saying, This is my beloved Son, in whom I am well pleased."

John 3:35 - "The Father loveth the Son, and hath given all things into his hand."

John 14:13 - "And whatsoever ye shall ask in my name, that will I do, that the Father may be glorified in the Son."

Romans 8:16 - "The Spirit itself beareth witness with our spirit, that we are the children of God:"

Romans 8:39 - "Nor height, nor depth, nor any other creature, shall be able to separate us from the love of God, which is in Christ Jesus our Lord."

Revelation 21:7 - "He that overcometh shall inherit all things; and I will be his God, and he shall be my son."

Sorrow

I trade my sorrows for Joy!

Psalm 13:2 - "How long shall I take counsel in my soul, having sorrow in my heart daily? how long shall mine enemy be exalted over me?"

Psalm 18:4-5 - "The sorrows of death compassed me, and the floods of ungodly men made me afraid. The sorrows of hell compassed me about: the snares of death prevented me."

Psalm 32:10 - "Many sorrows shall be to the wicked: but he that trusteth in the LORD, mercy shall compass him about."

Proverbs 10:22 - "The blessing of the LORD, it maketh rich, and he addeth no sorrow with it."

Ecclesiastes 7:3 - "Sorrow is better than laughter: for by the sadness of the countenance the heart is made better."

Isaiah 35:10 - "And the ransomed of the LORD shall return, and come to Zion with songs and everlasting joy upon their heads: they shall obtain joy and gladness, and sorrow and sighing shall flee away."

Soul Seeking
God seeks to save my soul!

Deuteronomy 4:29 - "But if from thence thou shalt seek the LORD thy God, thou shalt find him, if thou seek him with all thy heart and with all thy soul."

Psalm 25:1 - "Unto thee, O LORD, do I lift up my soul."

Psalm 42:1 - "As the hart panteth after the water brooks, so panteth my soul after thee, O God."

Psalm 63:1 - "O God, thou art my God; early will I seek thee: my soul thirsteth for thee, my flesh longeth for thee in a dry and thirsty land, where no water is;"

Psalm 139:23 - "Search me, O God, and know my heart: try me, and know my thoughts:"

Lamentations 3:25 - "The LORD is good unto them that wait for him, to the soul that seeketh him."

Isaiah 26:9 - "With my soul have I desired thee in the night; yea, with my spirit within me will I seek thee early: for when thy judgments are in the earth, the inhabitants of the world will learn righteousness."

Sowing
I will reap whatever I sow!

Leviticus 26:5 - "And your threshing shall reach unto the vintage, and the vintage shall reach unto the sowing time: and ye shall eat your bread to the full, and dwell in your land safely."

Psalm 126:5 - "They that sow in tears shall reap in joy."

Isaiah 61:11 - "For as the earth bringeth forth her bud, and as the garden causeth the things that are sown in it to spring forth; so the Lord GOD will cause righteousness and praise to spring forth before all the nations."

1 Corinthians 15:43-44 - "It is sown in dishonour; it is raised in glory: it is sown in weakness; it is raised in power: It is sown a natural body; it is raised a spiritual body. There is a natural body, and there is a spiritual body."

Galatians 6:7-8 - "Be not deceived; God is not mocked: for whatsoever a man soweth, that shall he also reap. For he that soweth to his flesh shall of the flesh reap corruption; but he that soweth to the Spirit shall of the Spirit reap life everlasting."

Spirit - Led
I am led by the Spirit of God!

Psalm 17:27 - "He that hath knowledge spareth his words: and a man of understanding is of an excellent spirit."

Isaiah 61:3 - "To appoint unto them that mourn in Zion, to give unto them beauty for ashes, the oil of joy for mourning, the garment of praise for the spirit of heaviness; that they might be called trees of righteousness, the planting of the LORD, that he might be glorified."

Luke 4:1 - "And Jesus being full of the Holy Ghost returned from Jordan, and was led by the Spirit into the wilderness,"

Romans 8:4 - "That the righteousness of the law might be fulfilled in us, who walk not after the flesh, but after the Spirit."

Romans 8:14 - "For as many as are led by the Spirit of God, they are the sons of God."

Galatians 5:18 - "But if ye be led of the Spirit, ye are not under the law."

Spirit of God
The Spirit of God lives inside me!

Job 33:4 - "The spirit of God hath made me, and the breath of the Almighty hath given me life."

Psalm 31:5 - "Into thine hand I commit my spirit: thou hast redeemed me, O LORD God of truth."

Psalm 51:10 - "Create in me a clean heart, O God; and renew a right spirit within me."

Psalm 143:10 - "Teach me to do thy will; for thou art my God: thy spirit is good; lead me into the land of uprightness."

Ecclesiastes 11:5 - "As thou knowest not what is the way of the spirit, nor how the bones do grow in the womb of her that is with child: even so thou knowest not the works of God who maketh all."

1 Corinthians 3:16 - "Know ye not that ye are the temple of God, and that the Spirit of God dwelleth in you?"

Romans 8:14 - "For as many as are led by the Spirit of God, they are the sons of God."

Spirit-Filled
I am anointed with God's spirit!

Exodus 31:3 - "And I have filled him with the spirit of God, in wisdom, and in understanding, and in knowledge, and in all manner of workmanship,"

Exodus 35:31 - "And he hath filled him with the spirit of God, in wisdom, in understanding, and in knowledge, and in all manner of workmanship;"

Luke 2:40 - "And the child grew, and waxed strong in spirit, filled with wisdom: and the grace of God was upon him."

Acts 2:4 - "And they were all filled with the Holy Ghost, and began to speak with other tongues, as the Spirit gave them utterance."

Romans 8:4 - "That the righteousness of the law might be fulfilled in us, who walk not after the flesh, but after the Spirit."

Ephesians 5:18 - "And be not drunk with wine, wherein is excess; but be filled with the Spirit;"

Colossians 1:9 - "For this cause we also, since the day we heard it, do not cease to pray for you, and to desire that ye might be filled with the knowledge of his will in all wisdom and spiritual understanding;"

Strength
God's strength is made perfect in weakness!

Deuteronomy 31:6 - "Be strong and of a good courage, fear not, nor be afraid of them: for the LORD thy God, he it is that doth go with thee; he will not fail thee, nor forsake thee."

Nehemiah 8:10 - "Then he said unto them, Go your way, eat the fat, and drink the sweet, and send portions unto them for whom nothing is prepared: for this day is holy unto our LORD: neither be ye sorry; for the joy of the LORD is your strength."

Job 36:5 - "Behold, God is mighty, and despiseth not any: he is mighty in strength and wisdom."

Psalm 18:32 - "It is God that girdeth me with strength, and maketh my way perfect."

Psalm 18:39 - "For thou hast girded me with strength unto the battle: thou hast subdued under me those that rose up against me."

Psalm 20:6 - "Now know I that the LORD saveth his anointed; he will hear him from his holy heaven with the saving strength of his right hand."

Psalm 27:14 - "Wait on the LORD: be of good courage, and he shall strengthen thine heart: wait, I say, on the LORD."

Psalm 73:26 - "My flesh and my heart faileth: but God is the strength of my heart, and my portion for ever."

Isaiah 40:31 - "But they that wait upon the LORD shall renew their strength; they shall mount up with wings as eagles; they shall run, and not be weary; and they shall walk, and not faint."

Daniel 10:18 - "Then there came again and touched me one like the appearance of a man, and he strengthened me,"

2 Corinthians 12:9 - "And he said unto me, My grace is sufficient for thee: for my strength is made perfect in weakness. Most gladly therefore will I rather glory in my infirmities, that the power of Christ may rest upon me."

Ephesians 3:20 - "Now unto him that is able to do exceeding abundantly above all that we ask or think, according to the power that worketh in us,"

Philippians 4:13 - "I can do all things through Christ which strengtheneth me."

Submission

Submission plants seeds of honor!

Romans 10:3 - "For they being ignorant of God's righteousness, and going about to establish their own righteousness, have not submitted themselves unto the righteousness of God."

Ephesians 5:21 - "Submitting yourselves one to another in the fear of God."

Hebrews 13:17 - "Obey them that have the rule over you, and submit yourselves: for they watch for your souls, as they that must give account, that they may do it with joy, and not with grief: for that is unprofitable for you."

James 4:7 - "Submit yourselves therefore to God. Resist the devil, and he will flee from you."

1 Peter 5:5 - "Likewise, ye younger, submit yourselves unto the elder. Yea, all of you be subject one to another, and be clothed with humility: for God resisteth the proud, and giveth grace to the humble."

1 Peter 2:13 - "Submit yourselves to every ordinance of man for the Lord's sake: whether it be to the king, as supreme;"

Suffering
Compassion grows with suffering!

Luke 18:7 - "And shall not God avenge his own elect, which cry day and night unto him, though he bear long with them?"

2 Corinthians 1:6-7 - "And whether we be afflicted, it is for your consolation and salvation, which is effectual in the enduring of the same sufferings which we also suffer... And our hope of you is stedfast, knowing, that as ye are partakers of the sufferings, so shall ye be also of the consolation."

2 Timothy 2:12 - "If we suffer, we shall also reign with him: if we deny him, he also will deny us:"

Hebrews 11:25 - "Choosing rather to suffer affliction with the people of God, than to enjoy the pleasures of sin for a season;"

1 Peter 3:17 - "For it is better, if the will of God be so, that ye suffer for well doing, than for evil doing."

1 Peter 4:19 - "Wherefore let them that suffer according to the will of God commit the keeping of their souls to him in well doing, as unto a faithful Creator."

𝒯emptation
God provides an escape from temptation!

Matthew 26:41 - "Watch and pray, that ye enter not into temptation: the spirit indeed is willing, but the flesh is weak."

Luke 11:4 - "And forgive us our sins; for we also forgive every one that is indebted to us. And lead us not into temptation; but deliver us from evil."

Luke 22:42 - "Saying, Father, if thou be willing, remove this cup from me: nevertheless not my will, but thine, be done."

Romans 14:13 - "Let us not therefore judge one another any more: but judge this rather, that no man put a stumblingblock or an occasion to fall in his brother's way."

1 Corinthians 10:13 - "There hath no temptation taken you but such as is common to man: but God is faithful, who will not suffer you to be tempted above that ye are able; but will with the temptation also make a way to escape, that ye may be able to bear it."

Galatians 6:1 - "Brethren, if a man be overtaken in a fault, ye which are spiritual, restore such an one in the spirit of meekness; considering thyself, lest thou also be tempted."

Hebrews 2:18 - "For in that he himself hath suffered being tempted, he is able to succour them that are tempted."

Hebrews 4:15 - "For we have not an high priest which cannot be touched with the feeling of our infirmities; but was in all points tempted like as we are, yet without sin."

James 1:2 - "My brethren, count it all joy when ye fall into divers temptations;"

James 1:12 - "Blessed is the man that endureth temptation: for when he is tried, he shall receive the crown of life, which the Lord hath promised to them that love him."

James 1:13-14 - "Let no man say when he is tempted, I am tempted of God: for God cannot be tempted with evil, neither tempteth he any man: But every man is tempted, when he is drawn away of his own lust, and enticed."

2 Peter 2:9 - "The Lord knoweth how to deliver the godly out of temptations, and to reserve the unjust unto the day of judgment to be punished:"

Revelation 3:10 - "Because thou hast kept the word of my patience, I also will keep thee from the hour of temptation, which shall come upon all the world, to try them that dwell upon the earth."

Thankful
I am thankful for all things!

Psalm 30:4 - "Sing unto the LORD, O ye saints of his, and give thanks at the remembrance of his holiness."

Psalm 69:30 - "I will praise the name of God with a song, and will magnify him with thanksgiving."

Psalm 100:4 - "Enter into his gates with thanksgiving, and into his courts with praise: be thankful unto him, and bless his name."

Luke 6:35 - "But love ye your enemies, and do good, and lend, hoping for nothing again; and your reward shall be great, and ye shall be the children of the Highest:"

2 Corinthians 4:15 - "For all things are for your sakes, that the abundant grace might through the thanksgiving of many redound to the glory of God."

Colossians 3:15 - "And let the peace of God rule in your hearts, to the which also ye are called in one body; and be ye thankful."

Thankfulness
I choose to be thankful!

1 Chronicles 16:34 - "O give thanks unto the LORD; for he is good; for his mercy endureth for ever."

Psalm 26:7 - "That I may publish with the voice of thanksgiving, and tell of all thy wondrous works."

Psalm 69:30 - "I will praise the name of God with a song, and will magnify him with thanksgiving."

Psalm 92:1 - "It is a good thing to give thanks unto the Lord, and to sing praises unto thy name, O most high:"

Psalm 119:62 - "At midnight I will rise to give thanks unto thee because of thy righteous judgments."

1 Corinthians 15:57 - "But thanks be to God, which giveth us the victory through our Lord Jesus Christ."

2 Corinthians 9:15 - "Thanks be unto God for his unspeakable gift."

1 Thessalonians 5:18 - "In every thing give thanks: for this is the will of God in Christ Jesus concerning you."

Tithe

Tithing brings provision for me!

Leviticus 27:30 - "And all the tithe of the land, whether of the seed of the land, or of the fruit of the tree, is the LORD's: it is holy unto the LORD."

Deuteronomy 14:22 - "Thou shalt truly tithe all the increase of thy seed, that the field bringeth forth year by year."

Proverbs 3:9 - "Honour the LORD with thy substance, and with the firstfruits of all thine increase:"

Malachi 3:10-11 - "Bring ye all the tithes into the storehouse, that there may be meat in mine house, and prove me now herewith, saith the LORD of hosts, if I will not open you the windows of heaven, and pour you out a blessing, that there shall not be room enough to receive it. And I will rebuke the devourer for your sakes, and he shall not destroy the fruits of your ground; neither shall your vine cast her fruit before the time in the field, saith the LORD of hosts."

Treasures

I have treasures in Heaven!

Proverbs 2:4 - *"If thou seekest her as silver, and searchest for her as for hid treasures;"*

Proverbs 8:21 - *"That I may cause those that love me to inherit substance; and I will fill their treasures."*

Proverbs 10:2 - *"Treasures of wickedness profit nothing: but righteousness delivereth from death."*

Isaiah 45:3 - *"And I will give thee the treasures of darkness, and hidden riches of secret places, that thou mayest know that I, the LORD, which call thee by thy name, am the God of Israel."*

Matthew 6:19-21 - *"Lay not up for yourselves treasures upon earth, where moth and rust doth corrupt, and where thieves break through and steal: But lay up for yourselves treasures in heaven, where neither moth nor rust doth corrupt, and where thieves do not break through nor steal: For where your treasure is, there will your heart be also."*

Colossians 2:3 - *"In whom are hid all the treasures of wisdom and knowledge."*

Trials

My trials strengthen me!

Romans 5:3-5 - *"And not only so, but we glory in tribulations also: knowing that tribulation worketh patience; And patience, experience; and experience, hope: And hope maketh not ashamed; because the love of God is shed abroad in our hearts by the Holy Ghost which is given unto us."*

2 Corinthians 8:2 - "How that in a great trial of affliction the abundance of their joy and their deep poverty abounded unto the riches of their liberality."

1 Peter 1:7 - "That the trial of your faith, being much more precious than of gold that perisheth, though it be tried with fire, might be found unto praise and honour and glory at the appearing of Jesus Christ:"

1 Peter 4:12-13 - "Beloved, think it not strange concerning the fiery trial which is to try you, as though some strange thing happened unto you: But rejoice, inasmuch as ye are partakers of Christ's sufferings; that, when his glory shall be revealed, ye may be glad also with exceeding joy."

1 Peter 4:16 - "Yet if any man suffer as a Christian, let him not be ashamed; but let him glorify God on this behalf."

Tribulation

Tribulation builds character!

Deuteronomy 4:30-31 - "When thou art in tribulation, and all these things are come upon thee, even in the latter days, if thou turn to the LORD thy God, and shalt be obedient unto his voice; (For the LORD thy God is a merciful God;) he will not forsake thee, neither destroy thee, nor forget the covenant of thy fathers which he sware unto them."

John 16:33 - "These things I have spoken unto you, that in me ye might have peace. In the world ye shall have tribulation: but be of good cheer; I have overcome the world."

Romans 8:35 - "Who shall separate us from the love of Christ? shall tribulation, or distress, or persecution, or famine, or nakedness, or peril, or sword?"

2 Corinthians 1:4 - "Who comforteth us in all our tribulation, that we may be able to comfort them which are in any trouble, by the comfort wherewith we ourselves are comforted of God."

Revelation 2:10 - "Fear none of those things which thou shalt suffer: behold, the devil shall cast some of you into prison, that ye may be tried; and ye shall have tribulation ten days: be thou faithful unto death, and I will give thee a crown of life."

Trust

My relationship builds trust in God!

Psalm 9:10 - "And they that know thy name will put their trust in thee: for thou, LORD, hast not forsaken them that seek thee."

Psalm 17:7 - "Shew thy marvellous lovingkindness, O thou that savest by thy right hand them which put their trust in thee from those that rise up against them."

Psalm 34:8 - "O taste and see that the LORD is good: blessed is the man that trusteth in him."

Psalm 73:28 - "But it is good for me to draw near to God: I have put my trust in the Lord GOD, that I may declare all thy works."

Psalm 118:8 - "It is better to trust in the LORD than to put confidence in man."

Proverbs 3:5-6 - "Trust in the LORD with all thine heart; and lean not unto thine own understanding. In all thy ways acknowledge him, and he shall direct thy paths."

Proverbs 30:5 - "Every word of God is pure: he is a shield unto them that put their trust in him."

Truth
Truth makes me free!

Psalm 31:5 - "Into thine hand I commit my spirit: thou hast redeemed me, O LORD God of truth."

Psalm 33:4 - "For the word of the LORD is right; and all his works are done in truth."

Psalm 40:11 - "Withhold not thou thy tender mercies from me, O LORD: let thy lovingkindness and thy truth continually preserve me."

Psalm 51:6 - "Behold, thou desirest truth in the inward parts: and in the hidden part thou shalt make me to know wisdom."

Psalm 85:11 - "Truth shall spring out of the earth; and righteousness shall look down from heaven."

Psalm 86:11 - "Teach me thy way, O LORD; I will walk in thy truth: unite my heart to fear thy name."

Psalm 100:5 - "For the LORD is good; his mercy is everlasting; and his truth endureth to all generations."

John 4:23 - "But the hour cometh, and now is, when the true worshippers shall worship the Father in spirit and in truth: for the Father seeketh such to worship him."

John 8:32 - "And ye shall know the truth, and the truth shall make you free."

John 14:17 - "Even the Spirit of truth; whom the world cannot receive, because it seeth him not, neither knoweth him: but ye know him; for he dwelleth with you, and shall be in you."

John 16:13 - "Howbeit when he, the Spirit of truth, is come, he will guide you into all truth: for he shall not speak of himself; but whatsoever he shall hear, that shall he speak: and he will shew you things to come."

John 17:17 - "Then said some of his disciples among themselves, What is this that he saith unto us, A little while, and ye shall not see me: and again, a little while, and ye shall see me: and, Because I go to the Father?"

Romans 7:15 - "For that which I do I allow not: for what I would, that do I not; but what I hate, that do I."

2 Corinthians 13:8 - "For we can do nothing against the truth, but for the truth."

Unity
I live in unity with God's people!

Psalm 100:2 - "Serve the LORD with gladness: come before his presence with singing."

Psalm 133:1 - "Behold, how good and how pleasant it is for brethren to dwell together in unity!"

Galatians 6:10 - "As we have therefore opportunity, let us do good unto all men, especially unto them who are of the household of faith."

Ephesians 4:3 - *"Endeavouring to keep the unity of the Spirit in the bond of peace."*

Ephesians 4:13 - *"Till we all come in the unity of the faith, and of the knowledge of the Son of God, unto a perfect man, unto the measure of the stature of the fulness of Christ:"*

Colossians 3:16 - *"Let the word of Christ dwell in you richly in all wisdom; teaching and admonishing one another in psalms and hymns and spiritual songs, singing with grace in your hearts to the Lord."*

Victory
I live in victory every day!

1 Chronicles 29:11 - *"Thine, O LORD is the greatness, and the power, and the glory, and the victory, and the majesty: for all that is in the heaven and in the earth is thine; thine is the kingdom, O LORD, and thou art exalted as head above all."*

Psalm 60:12 - *"Through God we shall do valiantly: for he it is that shall tread down our enemies."*

Psalm 89:18 - *"For the LORD is our defence; and the Holy One of Israel is our king."*

Psalm 98:1 - *"O sing unto the LORD a new song; for he hath done marvellous things: his right hand, and his holy arm, hath gotten him the victory."*

Psalm 118:17 - *"I shall not die, but live, and declare the works of the LORD."*

Isaiah 25:8 - "He will swallow up death in victory; and the Lord GOD will wipe away tears from off all faces; and the rebuke of his people shall he take away from off all the earth: for the LORD hath spoken it."

Micah 7:8 - "Rejoice not against me, O mine enemy: when I fall, I shall arise; when I sit in darkness, the LORD shall be a light unto me."

Romans 8:37 - "Nay, in all these things we are more than conquerors through him that loved us."

1 Corinthians 15:54 - "So when this corruptible shall have put on incorruption, and this mortal shall have put on immortality, then shall be brought to pass the saying that is written, Death is swallowed up in victory."

1 Corinthians 15:57 - "But thanks be to God, which giveth us the victory through our Lord Jesus Christ."

1 John 2:14 - "I have written unto you, fathers, because ye have known him that is from the beginning. I have written unto you, young men, because ye are strong, and the word of God abideth in you, and ye have overcome the wicked one."

1 John 5:4 - "For whatsoever is born of God overcometh the world: and this is the victory that overcometh the world, even our faith."

Revelation 12:11 - "And they overcame him by the blood of the Lamb, and by the word of their testimony; and they loved not their lives unto the death."

Vitality
I am filled with Vitality!

Deuteronomy 6:2 - "That thou mightest fear the LORD thy God, to keep all his statutes and his commandments, which I command thee, thou, and thy son, and thy son's son, all the days of thy life; and that thy days may be prolonged."

Philippians 4:8 - "Finally, brethren, whatsoever things are true, whatsoever things are honest, whatsoever things are just, whatsoever things are pure, whatsoever things are lovely, whatsoever things are of good report; if there be any virtue, and if there be any praise, think on these things."

Hebrews 6:1 - "Therefore leaving the principles of the doctrine of Christ, let us go on unto perfection; not laying again the foundation of repentance from dead works, and of faith toward God,"

War
I declare Peace!

Exodus 18:19 - "Hearken now unto my voice, I will give thee counsel, and God shall be with thee: Be thou for the people to God-ward, that thou mayest bring the causes unto God:"

Psalm 144:1 - "Blessed be the LORD my strength which teacheth my hands to war, and my fingers to fight:"

Ecclesiastes 3:8 - "A time to love, and a time to hate; a time of war, and a time of peace."

Ecclesiastes 9:18 - "Wisdom is better than weapons of war..."

Isaiah 41:12 - "Thou shalt seek them, and shalt not find them, even them that contended with thee: they that war against thee shall be as nothing, and as a thing of nought."

2 Corinthians 10:3-4 - "For though we walk in the flesh, we do not war after the flesh: (For the weapons of our warfare are not carnal, but mighty through God to the pulling down of strong holds;)"

Willingness
My spirit is willing!

Judges 5:2 - "Praise ye the LORD for the avenging of Israel, when the people willingly offered themselves."

Judges 5:9 - "...that offered themselves willingly among the people. Bless ye the LORD."

Proverbs 16:3 - "Commit thy works unto the LORD, and thy thoughts shall be established."

Isaiah 1:19 - "If ye be willing and obedient, ye shall eat the good of the land:"

Matthew 26:41 - "Watch and pray, that ye enter not into temptation: the spirit indeed is willing, but the flesh is weak."

Luke 22:42 - "Saying, Father, if thou be willing, remove this cup from me: nevertheless not my will, but thine, be done."

Galatians 5:25 - "If we live in the Spirit, let us also walk in the Spirit."

Hebrews 13:18 - "Pray for us: for we trust we have a good conscience, in all things willing to live honestly."

Wisdom

I will ask for Wisdom... the greatest gift of all!

Deuteronomy 11:26 - "Behold, I set before you this day a blessing and a curse;"

1 Kings 4:29 - "And God gave Solomon wisdom and understanding exceeding much, and largeness of heart, even as the sand that is on the sea shore."

1 Kings 4:30 - "And Solomon's wisdom excelled the wisdom of all the children of the east country, and all the wisdom of Egypt."

Psalm 37:30 - "The mouth of the righteous speaketh wisdom, and his tongue talketh of judgment."

Proverbs 1:5 - "A wise man will hear, and will increase learning; and a man of understanding shall attain unto wise counsels:"

Proverbs 2:6 - "For the LORD giveth wisdom: out of his mouth cometh knowledge and understanding."

Proverbs 2:11 - "Discretion shall preserve thee, understanding shall keep thee:"

Proverbs 3:13 - "Happy is the man that findeth wisdom, and the man that getteth understanding."

Proverbs 3:21-23 - "My son, let not them depart from thine eyes: keep sound wisdom and discretion. So shall they be life unto thy soul, and grace to thy neck. Then shalt thou walk in thy way safely, and thy foot shall not stumble."

Proverbs 13:20 - "A wise man will hear, and will increase learning; and a man of understanding shall attain unto wise counsels:"

Proverbs 15:2 - "The tongue of the wise useth knowledge aright: but the mouth of fools poureth out foolishness."

Proverbs 15:22 - "Without counsel purposes are disappointed: but in the multitude of counsellors they are established."

Proverbs 16:20 - "He that handleth a matter wisely shall find good: and whoso trusteth in the LORD, happy is he."

Proverbs 16:23 - "The heart of the wise teacheth his mouth, and addeth learning to his lips."

Proverbs 24:5 - "A wise man is strong; yea, a man of knowledge increaseth strength."

Proverbs 28:26 - " He that trusteth in his own heart is a fool: but whoso walketh wisely, he shall be delivered."

Ecclesiastes 5:2 - "Be not rash with thy mouth, and let not thine heart be hasty to utter any thing before God: for God is in heaven, and thou upon earth: therefore let thy words be few."

Isaiah 65:16 - "That he who blesseth himself in the earth shall bless himself in the God of truth; and he that sweareth in the earth shall swear by the God of truth; because the former troubles are forgotten, and because they are hid from mine eyes."

1 Corinthians 2:13 - "Which things also we speak, not in the words which man's wisdom teacheth, but which the Holy Ghost teacheth; comparing spiritual things with spiritual."

Ephesians 6:12 - "For we wrestle not against flesh and blood, but against principalities, against powers, against the rulers of the darkness of this world, against spiritual wickedness in high places."

Colossians 3:16 - "Forbearing one another, and forgiving one another, if any man have a quarrel against any: even as Christ forgave you, so also do ye."

James 1:5 - "If any of you lack wisdom, let him ask of God, that giveth to all men liberally, and upbraideth not; and it shall be given him."

James 1:19 - "Wherefore, my beloved brethren, let every man be swift to hear, slow to speak, slow to wrath:"

James 3:10 - "Out of the same mouth proceedeth blessing and cursing. My brethren, these things ought not so to be."

James 3:17 - "But the wisdom that is from above is first pure, then peaceable, gentle, and easy to be intreated, full of mercy and good fruits, without partiality, and without hypocrisy."

Psalm 37:30 - "The mouth of the righteous speaketh wisdom, and his tongue talketh of judgment."

Psalm 111:10 - "The fear of the LORD is the beginning of wisdom: a good understanding have all they that do his commandments: his praise endureth for ever."

Proverbs 15:22 - "Without counsel purposes are disappointed: but in the multitude of counsellors they are established."

Romans 14:2 - "For one believeth that he may eat all things: another, who is weak, eateth herbs."

Worry
Worry does not profit me today!

Ecclesiastes 3:11 - "He hath made every thing beautiful in his time: also he hath set the world in their heart, so that no man can find out the work that God maketh from the beginning to the end."

Psalm 9:9 - "The LORD also will be a refuge for the oppressed, a refuge in times of trouble."

Psalm 9:13 - "Have mercy upon me, O LORD; consider my trouble which I suffer of them that hate me, thou that liftest me up from the gates of death:"

Psalm 27:5 - "For in the time of trouble he shall hide me in his pavilion: in the secret of his tabernacle shall he hide me; he shall set me up upon a rock."

Psalm 32:7 - "Thou art my hiding place; thou shalt preserve me from trouble; thou shalt compass me about with songs of deliverance. Selah."

Luke 10:41 - "And Jesus answered and said unto her, Martha, Martha, thou art careful and troubled about many things:"

Worship
I worship in God's presence!

Exodus 34:14 - "For thou shalt worship no other god: for the Lord, Whose name is Jealous, is a jealous God."

Psalm 29:2 - "Give unto the Lord the glory due unto His name; worship the Lord in the beauty of holiness."

Psalm 45: 11 - "So shall the king greatly desire thy beauty: for he is thy Lord; and worship thou him."

Psalm 96:9 - "O worship the LORD in the beauty of holiness: fear before him, all the earth."

Psalm 99:5 - "Exalt ye the LORD our God, and worship at his footstool; for he is holy."

Psalm 138:2 - "I will worship toward thy holy temple, and praise thy name for thy lovingkindness and for thy truth: for thou hast magnified thy word above all thy name."

John 4:23-24 - "But the hour cometh, and now is, when the true worshippers shall worship the Father in spirit and in truth: for the Father seeketh such to worship him. God is a Spirit: and they that worship him must worship him in spirit and in truth."

Definitions of Abuse

This information has been compiled (slightly modified for the reader) by the Domestic Abuse Intervention Project.

The continuous cycles of violence reveal manipulation with misuse of Power and Control at the center. If you recognize an abundance of the following characteristics in your own life, you too may be a victim of abuse.

Using Economic Abuse: Preventing you from getting or keeping a job; making you ask for money; giving you an allowance; taking your money; not letting you know about or have access to family income.

Using Male Privileges: Treating you like a servant; making all the big decisions; acting like the "master of the castle;" being the one to define men's and women's roles.

Using Children: Making you feel guilty about the children; using the children to relay messages; using visitation to harass you; threatening to take the children away.

Minimizing, Denying, and Blaming: Making light of the abuse and not taking your concerns about it seriously; saying the abuse didn't happen; shifting responsibility for abusive behavior; saying you caused it.

Using Isolation: Controlling what you do, whom you see and talk to, what you read, where you go; limiting your outside involvement; using jealousy to justify actions.

Using Emotional Abuse: Putting you down; making you feel bad about yourself; calling you names; making you think you're crazy; playing mind games; humiliating you; making you feel guilty.

Using Intimidation: Making you afraid by using looks, actions, gestures; smashing things; destroying your property; abusing pets; displaying weapons.

Using Coercion and Threats: Making and/or carrying out threats to do something to hurt you; threatening to leave you, to commit suicide, to report you to welfare; making you drop charges; making you do illegal things.

READING FAVORITES

ABC Woman Finds Freedom
Compiled by Kathleen Schubitz

ABCs of Who I Am in Christ!
by Kathleen Schubitz

Amazing Grace for Widows
by Jane C. Wittbold

Finding Purpose after Abuse
Exposing enemy lies to empower believers with God's truth
by Kathleen Schubitz

God's New Wine
by Kathleen Schubitz

His Heart Calls
Love Notes from God's Word
by Kathleen Schubitz

If the Battle is the Lord's... Why Am I So Tired?
by Randy Newberry

...In His Presence (B/W & Color)
by Kathleen Schubitz

Jesus Invites You...to the Marriage Supper of the Lamb
by Jane C. Wittbold

Lord, I Praise You...*Sowing seeds of gratitude*
by Kathleen Schubitz

Lord, I Worship You...
by Kathleen Schubitz

Order in the House!
by Virginia Mendes

Personal Poetic Promises from God's Word
by Kathleen Schubitz

Poetry: Healing for the soul (vol 1)
by Kathleen Schubitz

Poetry: Healing for the soul (vol 2)
by Kathleen Schubitz

* * * * * * * * * * * * * *

Visit us through Amazon or our online bookstore:
www.rpjandco.com

KATHLEEN SCHUBITZ is an accomplished author, poet, speaker and business woman. God's spoken word from Romans 14:17 birthed RPJ & Company (Righteousness, Peace and Joy) in 2004, thereby establishing a Kingdom publishing business for God's people. As founder and president, her faith in God and desire to follow His leading  compels her to pursue her own writing and publish books, devotionals, poetry, calendars and marketing materials for leaders and Kingdom writers.

After growing up in the Midwestern United States, Kathleen presently resides in central Florida. Preparation for her calling comes from serving at Rotary International headquarters as production assistant for *The Rotarian* magazine. Having now become an inspirational writer, she lives a life of dedication to God, choosing to turn life's hardships into stepping stones for success. Pressing through an oppressive childhood, life-threatening abuse and sickness as an adult, Kathleen allows the Spirit of God to turn her tragedies into triumph and devastation into dedication. Victorious over her own hurtful situations, she now helps others discover truth to live a life of freedom.

A few of Kathleen's published works include the following: *...In His Presence, Scripture Keys, His Heart Calls, Personal Poetic Promises from God's Word* and *ABCs of Who I Am in Christ!* Her prolific skills in writing, proof-editing, design and typography help new and experienced authors publish books and quality products with a spirit of excellence. To learn more about Kathleen Schubitz or publishing and related services by RPJ & Company, visit: RPJandco.com.

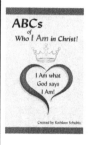

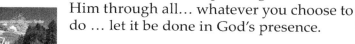
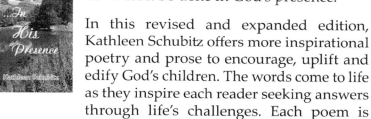

Personal Poetic Promises from God's Word

A devotional of personal promises (126) written in free style poetry form to encourage every reader any time of day. Designed with a flower border for reading enjoyment. Complete with scripture verses. Makes a great gift for any occasion. B/W book - 4 x 6 - 72 pages. Also available in 5.25 x 8.25 color booklet form.

Poetry: Healing for the soul
Volume 1

Determined to expose and uproot the cause of wounds and years of struggle, the author touches the heart and soul in a personal way. Transformed by her search for freedom and wholeness, her insight brings hope and healing to others. Scripture verses are included for further study and personal reflection.

Poetry: Healing for the soul
Volume 2

Continuing her pursuit of truth and God's love, the poet shares her intimate moments through writing and inspiration. With a ready pen and heart, more verses are sure to touch the reader's heart.

Printed in Great Britain
by Amazon

19594619R00088